Headway

Academic Skills

Listening, Speaking, and Study Skills

LEVEL 1 **Student's Book**

Emma and Gary Pathare
Series Editors: Liz and John Soars

OXFORD

CONTENTS

1 Starting out

LISTENING SKILLS Listening for specific information • Listening for gist
SPEAKING SKILLS Checking and confirming information • Sentence stress
VOCABULARY DEVELOPMENT What can we learn? • Functional language • Letter names

LISTENING Listening at college

1 Look at the photos. Work with a partner. Match the people with the information they give you at college.

1 ☐ instructions for registration
2 ☐ formal prepared talks
3 ☐ advice and feedback on a project
4 ☐ advice on borrowing books and doing research
5 ☐ classroom instructions

lecturer

tutor

admin officer

teacher

librarian

2 🎧 1.1 Listen to the teacher giving instructions. Ⓒircle the correct answer.

1 Turn to page **28 / 38 / 48**.
2 Finish the exercise in **5 / 15 / 50** minutes.
3 Work **in pairs / alone / in a group**.

3 **Read STUDY SKILL** 🎧 1.2 Look at the student's notes. Listen to the conversation and complete the notes.

Important college information
ID number – _____
Room number – _____
Computer studies course code – _____

STUDY SKILL Listening for specific information

We often listen for specific information, e.g. names or numbers. When you are listening for specific information:

- decide what information you need before you listen.
- read the questions you have to answer carefully.
- focus your listening on the information you need.
- write down the key information.

4 🔘 1.3 Listen to three announcements. What is the general idea of each one? Match a–c with announcements 1–3.

a ☐ choosing a talk
b ☐ buying / collecting something
c ☐ giving information

Life as a college student

5 **Read STUDY SKILL** 🔘 1.4 Listen to the start of Dr Lewis's lecture about college life. Which sentence gives a summary of each part of the lecture?

1 a Dr Lewis wants students to enjoy college.
   b College life is not the same as school life.

2 a You need to work independently at college.
   b It's best to work in the library.

3 a The most important thing is to pass your exams.
   b Students should work hard at all times.

4 a You should behave like an adult.
   b You must hand in your work on time.

> **STUDY SKILL** Listening for gist
>
> Sometimes we listen for *gist*, i.e. general meaning. When you are listening for gist:
> - look at pictures, visuals, and titles before listening.
> - don't worry about details. Listen for the main idea.

6 🔘 1.4 Some colleges have contracts between the college and the student. Listen again and complete the contract.

STUDENT CONTRACT

Working independently

- learn to use the _____
- read _____
- check _____
- ask _____
- find out _____

Completing work

- care about _____
- work hard _____

Being professional

- be interested in _____
- behave _____
- arrive _____
- hand in your work _____

---

7 Work with a partner. Write five differences between college and school.

8 Work in a group. Decide on the three biggest differences between college and school.

SPEAKING Checking information

1 Work with a partner. What information do you need when you start college? Where can you get the information?

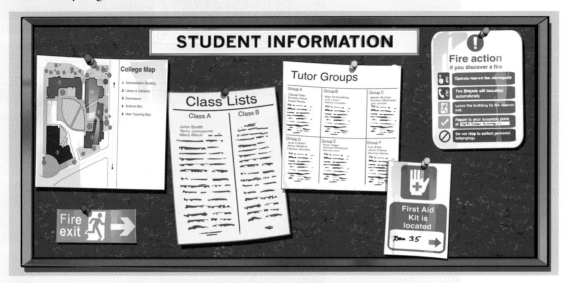

2 Match the questions with the answers.

1	What's your English teacher's name?	a	It's in room D4.
2	Which room is the English class in?	b	It's HS 45772.
3	Could you tell me where the cafeteria is?	c	Mr Price.
4	What's your ID number?	d	It's next to the library.

3 1.5 Listen and check your answers.

4 Work with a partner. Write four similar questions, then ask and answer them.

5 **Read STUDY SKILL** 1.6 Listen to the complete conversation. How many questions did the student ask?

> **STUDY SKILL** Checking and confirming information
>
> You can ask questions to check information.
> *Can you say that again, please?*
>
> People can ask you questions to confirm information. You can use polite expressions when you reply.
> *Yes, that's right.*
> *I'm afraid that's wrong.*

6 1.6 Read the expressions in the Language Bank. Listen to the conversation again. Tick (✓) the expressions you hear.

> **LANGUAGE BANK** Checking and confirming
>
> | Checking | Confirming |
> |---|---|
> | *Can you spell that, please?* | *Yes, that's right.* |
> | *Can you repeat that, please?* | *No, it's …* |
> | *Can you say that again, please?* | *No, that's not right.* |
> | *Did you say …?* | *I'm afraid that's wrong.* |
> | *Is this/that right?* | |

7 `Read STUDY SKILL` 🔊 **1.7** Listen to the expressions. <u>Underline</u> the stressed syllables.

1 Can you spell that, please?
2 Can you repeat that, please?
3 Can you say that again, please?
4 Did you say 'three'?
5 Is this right?
6 Yes, that's right.
7 No, it's 'seven' not 'eight'.
8 No, that's not right.
9 I'm afraid that's wrong.

8 🔊 **1.7** Listen again and repeat.

9 Look at the student ID card. Then complete ID card **a** with your details.

STUDY SKILL Sentence stress

In English, we stress the important words when we speak.

It's <u>next</u> to the <u>library</u>.

Can you <u>spell</u> that, <u>please</u>?

Stressed words and syllables are longer and louder.

Student ID Number	7569033
Department	Business
Course code	Eng 3341
Tutor	J Smith

a

PHOTO

Student ID Number _____

Department _____

Course code _____

Tutor _____

b

PHOTO

Student ID Number _____

Department _____

Course code _____

Tutor _____

10 Work with a partner. Ask questions and complete ID card **b** with information about your partner.

VOCABULARY DEVELOPMENT   What is vocabulary?

1 Read STUDY SKILL Use the words and expressions in the box to complete the table.

STUDY SKILL What can we learn?

When we learn vocabulary, we can learn:
- single words, e.g. *college, student, advice*
- multi-word items, e.g. *get up, phone number*
- expressions, e.g. *Yes, that's right.*

information	Yes, that's right.	look for	course code
Can you repeat that, please?		teacher	room number
I'm afraid that's wrong.	Did you say …?		independently

single words	multi-word items	expressions
information		

2 Read STUDY SKILL 🎵 1.6 Look at the expressions in the table and tick (✓) the correct function. Then listen to the conversation again to check.

	Checking	Confirming	Asking for help	Giving advice
Can you give me …?				
Is that right?				
Could you tell me …?				
Yes, that's right.				
Can you repeat that, please?				
I think you should …				
Can you spell that, please?				

STUDY SKILL Functional language

We often use expressions as *functional language*, for example:
- checking information, e.g. *Is this right?*
- confirming information, e.g. *Yes, that's right.*
- asking for help, e.g. *Could you help me, please?*
- giving advice, e.g. *I think you should …*

3 Read STUDY SKILL 🎵 1.8 Listen and repeat the letters.

4 🎵 1.9 Listen and complete the information.

MY TEACHERS	
Business 151	_____
Maths 177	_____ / _____
English 163	_____

STUDY SKILL Letter names

In the English alphabet there are 26 letters.

a b c d e f g h i j k l m n o p q r s t u v w x y z

Five of them are vowels: *a, e, i, o, u.*

The rest are consonants: *b, c d, f …*

5 Work in a group. Ask for the other students' names, and ask where they come from. Check the spelling and write the information down.

REVIEW

1 🎧 1.10 Listen and match speakers *a–d* with the types of information 1–6. There are two types of information you do not need.

1 ☐ feedback on a project
2 ☐ information about timetables
3 ☐ advice on how to research
4 ☐ announcements
5 ☐ instructions for registration
6 ☐ classroom instructions

2 🎧 1.10 Listen again and write the person who is speaking.

tutor	admin officer	librarian	teacher

a _____   c _____
b _____   d _____

3 🎧 1.11 Listen and complete the information on the registration form.

> ### City College
> ### Registration Form
>
> **Student information**
> First name:
> Surname: Marley
> Date of birth: 09/03/1992
> Full-time / Part-time:
> ID number:
>
> **Course information**
> Maths course code:
> English course code:
>
> **Contact details**
> Email: smarley@citycollege.ac
> Mobile:

4 Complete the sentences with the words in the box.

say	afraid	right	spell	help	should

1 Can you _____ that, please?
2 'Your ID number is 762004, isn't it?'
   'No, I'm _____ that's wrong.'
3 Could you _____ me, please?
4 Can you _____ that again, please?
5 I think you _____ talk to your tutor.
6 'Are you studying English?' 'Yes, that's _____ .'

2 Academic life

LISTENING SKILLS Predicting • Asking questions (1) • Giving a summary
SPEAKING SKILLS Finding out more and speaking for longer • Asking questions (2)
VOCABULARY DEVELOPMENT Organizing vocabulary (1) and (2)

LISTENING Academic routines

1 Here are some important things in college life.
How important is each one in your opinion?
Decide between Very important (✓✓),
Important (✓), or Not very important (✗).

1 group work
2 assessment
3 independent work
4 tutorials
5 free time
6 seminars

2 Work with a partner. Compare your answers.

3 🔊 2.1 Listen to the introduction to a seminar.
Tick (✓) two main points of the introduction.

The tutor wants the students to:

☐ be relaxed.
☐ come to every seminar.
☐ know about their new course.
☐ discuss ideas.

Students in Seoul, South Korea

4 🔊 2.1 Listen again and answer the questions.

1 What is the tutor's name? _____
2 How many students are in class today? _____
3 In a seminar, who can speak? _____

5 **Read STUDY SKILL** Work with a partner. Read some questions which students
will ask, and predict the tutor's answers.

Questions	Answers
How are we assessed?	
When do we do independent work?	
When do we have free time?	

6 🔊 2.2 Listen and check your predictions.

> **STUDY SKILL** Predicting
>
> To help you to understand a listening
> text, try to predict what it is about before
> you listen. To help you predict:
> - look at the title and pictures.
> - think about what you already know
>   about the topic.

7 ⊚ 2.3 Listen to three more questions that students ask. Make notes on the tutor's responses.

Questions	Answers
Do we have to buy any books?	
Who do I ask if I need help with my independent work?	
When we work in a group, can we choose who we work with?	

8 Work with a partner. Answer the questions in exercises 5 and 7 about your college.

9 Read **STUDY SKILL** ⊚ 2.4 Listen and write down the questions.

1 _____

2 _____

3 _____

4 _____

STUDY SKILL Asking questions (1)

In English, some words are stressed, and others are unstressed.
How are we *assessed*?
When do we have *free time*?
Unstressed words are shorter and quieter than stressed words.

10 ⊚ 2.4 <u>Underline</u> the stressed words and syllables in the questions in exercise 9. Then listen again, check, and repeat.

11 ⊚ 2.5 Listen to Kaoru giving Maha a summary of the seminar. Tick (✓) the things that Kaoru mentions.

☐ assessment ☐ planning time
☐ college website ☐ books
☐ number of lectures ☐ independent work

Kaoru   Maha

12 Read **STUDY SKILL** ⊚ 2.5 Listen again. Does Kaoru give a good summary? Why? Why not?

STUDY SKILL Giving a summary

We often give a summary of something we listen to. To give an effective summary, you should:
■ decide on the most important points.
■ think about the speaker's opinion of the subject.
■ keep the summary short and simple.

SPEAKING Talking about the college environment

1 Some students are asking questions. What are the questions about? Write the correct topics.

| library   lectures   projects   assessments   presentations |

1 How often do we attend these?
   Where do we go to attend these?   _____

2 How many books can we borrow?
   What time does it open?   _____

3 How often do we have to give them?
   Who do we give them to?   _____

4 Do we only have these at the end of term?
   What type do we get?   _____

5 Do we do these in groups or alone?
   How long do we get to complete them?   _____

2 Work with a partner. Ask and answer the questions in exercise 1 about your college.

3 Read the Rule. Put the words in the correct order to make questions.

1 you / How / do / lectures / often / ? / have   _____
2 work / When / ? / do / you / do / independent   _____
3 do / What / do / every / you / ? / day   _____
4 work / do / Where / independent /you / ? / do   _____
5 do / Where / have / you / ? / tutorials   _____

4 ◎ 2.6 Listen and check your answers.

5 Work with a partner. Ask and answer the questions in exercise 3.

6 **Read STUDY SKILL** Work with a partner. Ask and answer these questions. When you answer, add more information.

1 Do you drive to college?
2 Do you study English?
3 Do you do sports at college?
4 Does your day start early?
5 Do you study in the library?

> **RULE** Question forms
>
> To ask about daily routines, we use questions in the present simple.
>   *Where do you study?*
>   *How do you get to college?*
>
> This is the form of the questions:
>   *Wh- question word + do/does + subject + verb + …?*

STUDY SKILL Finding out more and speaking for longer

What is the difference between these two questions?
Where do you study?
Do you study in the library?

Questions with *Wh-* question words often get answers with more information.
'Where do you study?' 'When I am at college, I study in the coffee shop, but I prefer studying at home.'

Yes/No questions can make a conversation short.
'Do you study in the library?' 'No.'

To give longer answers to *Yes/No* questions, you must add more information.
No, I prefer studying at home, or in the coffee shop if I am at college.

7 **Read STUDY SKILL** 2.7 Listen and write the questions in the correct column.

Wh- questions	Yes/No questions

8 2.7 Listen again. <u>Underline</u> the stressed words and mark the intonation.

9 Work with a partner. Ask and answer the questions in exercise 7.

LANGUAGE BANK *How often ...?*

How often do we have a tutorial?	every	day
How often does the library open at the weekend?	once a	week
	twice a	fortnight
	three times a	month
		year

10 Read the expressions in the Language Bank. Work with a partner. Ask questions to find out if your partner is a good language learner.

ARE YOU A GOOD LANGUAGE LEARNER?

What do you do outside the classroom to help with your English? Do you ...?

	Yes	No	How often?
look at English websites	☐	☐	_____
read newspapers or magazines in English	☐	☐	_____
watch films in English	☐	☐	_____
have conversations in English	☐	☐	_____
listen to the radio in English	☐	☐	_____
revise grammar	☐	☐	_____
learn vocabulary	☐	☐	_____

11 Compare your answers with your partner's answers. Are you a good language learner?

VOCABULARY DEVELOPMENT Keeping a record

1 Match the ways of recording vocabulary with the pictures.

1 using a set of cards
2 using a wallchart
3 keeping a notebook
4 using a computer
5 recording yourself

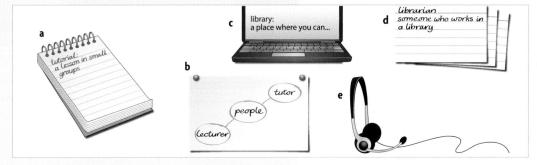

2 What are the advantages and disadvantages of methods 1–5 in exercise 1?
Which one works well for you?

3 Read STUDY SKILL Complete the two sub-topics, *places* and *work* on the
diagram opposite, with the college vocabulary in the box.

library	essay	project	lecture hall

STUDY SKILL Organizing vocabulary (1)

Topics and sub-topics

classroom presentation library project lab essay lecture hall cafeteria

You can use sub-topics to help you to organize the words more, e.g. sub-topics for
college are *places* and *work*:

topic	sub-topic	vocabulary
college	places	library, lecture hall ...
	work	essay ...

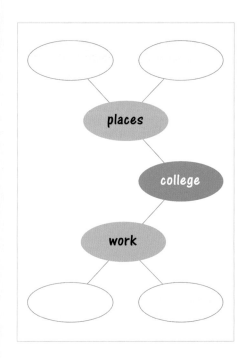

4 Work with a partner. Add more words to the diagram.

5 Read STUDY SKILL Complete the table with the words.

~~tutor/tutorial~~
lecture hall/to lecture/lecturer/lecture
library/librarian
presenter/presentation/to present

to learn/learner
study room/student/to study
admin department/admin officer

College vocabulary			
Places	Class type / activity	People	Verbs
	tutorial	tutor	

STUDY SKILL
Organizing vocabulary (2)

Word families

It is a good idea to record and learn the
words from a word family together:

A librarian is a person who works in a
library.

REVIEW

1 🔘 2.8 Listen to the start of a tutorial. Answer the questions.

  1 What is the main purpose of the tutorial?
    a to introduce the tutor
    b to give instructions for an assignment
    c to review this week's lectures

  2 When will the tutor give details of the next assignment?
    a in next week's tutorial
    b at the start of this tutorial
    c at the end of this tutorial

2 You are going to listen to another part of a tutorial. Predict the order the tutor will advise the students to follow when doing assignments.

  ☐ do the research
  ☐ write up the reports
  ☐ decide on the focus
  ☐ submit the assignments on Tuesday
  ☐ divide up the research tasks
  ☐ put the assignments in a folder
  ☐ discuss the notes

3 🔘 2.9 Listen and check your answers.

4 A student needs some information about life at college. Look at the student's notes and write the questions to find out the missing information.

TUTORIALS		
how many a week?	1	
room number?	2	
ASSIGNMENTS		
number of essays to write a term?	3	
submit – email, paper …?	4	
PRESENTATIONS		
use PowerPoint?	5	
always in groups?	6	

5 <u>Underline</u> the stressed syllables and mark the intonation in the questions that you wrote in exercise 4.

6 Work with a partner. Do a role-play between a student and a tutor. Ask and answer the questions. Use your own information and ideas when you answer.

3 Caring for the environment

LISTENING SKILLS Taking notes (1) and (2)
SPEAKING SKILLS Talking about numbers (1) and (2) • Word stress in numbers • Presentations (1)
RESEARCH Choosing a focus (1) and (2)

LISTENING Working together

1 Work with a partner. Answer the questions.

1 What do you know about *Earth Hour*?
2 What can you tell from the poster? What are the key words?
   What does the picture tell you?
3 What do you want to know about *Earth Hour*? Write three questions.

2 | Read STUDY SKILL | Read the introduction to the talk and ⟨circle⟩ the key words.
Then find a key word that Dr Smith explains.

Hello, I'm Dr Andrew Smith, professor of Environmental Studies at Braunton University. Today I'm here to talk about a global event called *Earth Hour* – I'm sure some of you have heard of it, right? Well, the global success of *Earth Hour* shows that ordinary people all over the world really want to stop pollution – by ordinary people, I mean people like you and me. For those of you who don't know, let me tell you a little bit about *Earth Hour* before I explain why I think it is such an important event.

3 ⊚ 3.1 Read and listen to the introduction. Does Dr Smith stress the key words?

4 ⊚ 3.2 Listen to the rest of the talk. ⟨Circle⟩ the key words for each part of the talk in the table.

Part	Key words	Main point
1	⟨global⟩ ⟨event⟩ ⟨important⟩ ⟨Earth Hour⟩ people	*Earth Hour is an important global event.*
2	Sydney 2007 plan turn off lights one hour March	
3	stop millions people switch off laughing	
4	growing media publicity famous buildings	
5	important unites people certainly computer	

5 Work with a partner. Use the key words and write the main points in the table.

EARTH HOUR
Lecture and discussion

Are you worried about the environment?
Do you want to 'go green'?

Talk by Dr Andrew Smith
Room B24 Tuesday 17th 2 p.m.

STUDY SKILL Taking notes (1)

When you are listening to a talk or lecture, try to identify the key words which give you the most important information.

Key words are often repeated and stressed.

Sometimes speakers explain or give examples to show what the key words mean.

media → *newspapers, TV, radio*

Always make a note of key words you hear.

Listening for numbers

6 Read the questions in the table below. Choose a type of answer from the box for each question and write it in the table.

number	length of time	year

Questions	Type of answer	Answers
1 In what year did Earth Hour start?	year	
2 How long do people turn off the lights for?		
3 How many people turned off their lights in the first year?		
4 How many people were involved in 2008?		
5 How many cities were involved in 2009?		
6 How many countries were involved in 2010?		

7 **Read STUDY SKILL** ☉ 3.3 Listen to parts 2 and 3 of the talk again. Add the answers to the table in exercise 6.

STUDY SKILL Taking notes (2)

Numbers
You need to be fast when you take notes about numbers.
- use figures, not words: 2   15
- use abbreviations: m for *million*
                          h for *hour*
                          min for *minutes*

Years
Look at how we say years:
2012   *twenty twelve*
1987   *nineteen eighty-seven*
1800   *eighteen hundred*

8 ☉ 3.4 Listen to a student giving a summary of the talk about *Earth Hour*. Write the numbers he gives in the table.

Information	Student answer
the year Earth Hour started	
how long people turn lights off for	
the number of people who turned off their lights in the first year	
the number of countries involved in 2010	

9 Compare the student's answers with your answers in exercise 6. Which answer did he get wrong?

7

28

126

2018

1964

2,000,000

SPEAKING Talking about numbers

1 🎧 3.5 Listen to a presenter talking about China. Write the numbers.

number of ...	answer
bicycles in China	
towns in China	
cities in China	
Chinese people travelling to work by bicycle	
bicycles in the bike park	

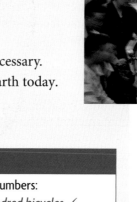

2 **Read STUDY SKILL** Put -s on *thousand* and *million* where necessary.
1 There are million of types of plants and animals on Earth today.
2 There are over four million types of insect.
3 The Earth has thousand of types of birds.
4 The Earth has over five thousand types of mammal.

> ### STUDY SKILL Talking about numbers (1)
>
> We don't add -s to *hundred*, *thousand*, and *million* when we say numbers:
> *four million cars* ✓   *two thousand people* ✓   *three hundred bicycles* ✓
>
> However, when we don't say an exact number, we add -s and we use *of*:
> *millions of cars* ✓   *thousands of people* ✓   *hundreds of bicycles* ✓

3 🎧 3.6 Listen and check your answers. Practise saying the sentences.

4 **Read STUDY SKILL** Look at the chart and complete the sentences.
1 _____ 90 million people in the Philippines.
2 _____ 80 million people in Germany.
3 Ethiopia _____ a population of _____ 80 million.
4 Egypt _____ a population of _____ 80 million.
5 Vietnam _____ a population of _____ 85 million.

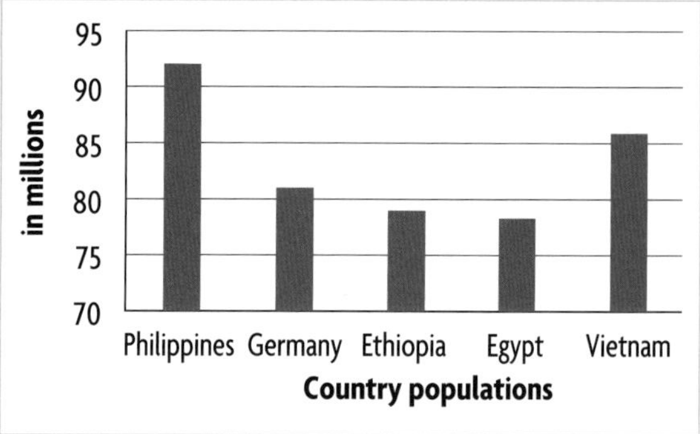

> ### STUDY SKILL Talking about numbers (2)
>
> We can use *there is/there are* and *has/have* to talk about numbers.
>
> *There is one Earth Hour event every year.*
> *They have fifteen minutes for questions.*
>
> Sometimes it is not necessary or possible to give an exact number. We can say:
>
> *about/around two hundred*   *under/fewer than fifty ...*
> *almost/nearly a million.*   *over/more than a thousand ...*
>
> *There are more than 60 million people in the United Kingdom.*
> *South Africa has a population of almost 50 million.*

Country populations (chart, in millions): Philippines ~92, Germany ~81, Ethiopia ~79, Egypt ~78, Vietnam ~86.

5 Work with a partner. Look at the chart in exercise 4. Ask and answer
questions. about the population in different countries.

'How many people live in Germany?'
'There are about 80 million people in Germany.'

6 **Read STUDY SKILL** 🔊 3.7 Listen and <u>underline</u> the numbers you hear.

1 There are about **thirteen / thirty**.
2 It has around **sixteen / sixty**.
3 They have nearly **seventeen / seventy**.
4 They have **nineteen / ninety**.
5 There are more than **sixteen /sixty**.
6 It has fewer than **fifteen / fifty**.
7 It has almost **eighteen / eighty**.
8 There are under **fifteen / fifty**.

7 Work with a partner. Take turns to say a sentence from exercise 6, choosing one of the numbers. Your partner must decide which number you are saying.

Giving a presentation

8 Work in a group. Look at the photos and notes. What environmental problems do they show? What other environmental problems can you think of?

9 Work with a partner. Choose an environmental problem. Write down the key words and three main points for this problem.

10 Make a poster about the problem you have chosen. Include some notes.

11 **Read STUDY SKILL** <u>Underline</u> the stress on your key words. Practise saying the words. Now say the words without looking at them.

> **STUDY SKILL** Presentations (1)
>
> In a presentation, key words are the most important words. They tell the audience what the important information and ideas are.
>
> To give a good presentation, you need to:
> - decide on your key words.
> - repeat the key words clearly.
>
> To say the key words well, you need to:
> - mark the stress, for example: en<u>vi</u>ronment.
> - practise saying the words.
>
> To find out how to mark the stress, you can:
> - check in a dictionary.
> - ask your teacher.

12 Work in a group. Show your poster and give a short presentation. Listen to the other presentations. Are the key words clear?

> **STUDY SKILL** Word stress in numbers
>
> Some pairs of different numbers sound almost the same. The main difference is the stress. What is the difference in stress between *15* and *50*?
>
> Look at the numbers:
>
> 15   fif<u>teen</u>
> 50   <u>fif</u>ty
>
> Which other pairs of numbers are similar?

- Only 20,000 polar bears worldwide.
- By 2050 two thirds will disappear.
- Threats – melting sea ice from climate change.

- 1960 – 122 million cars worldwide.
- 2010 – over 800 million.
- By 2020, possibly over 2 billion.

- Over 60% living species are in rainforests.
- They absorb CO_2 – they are the 'lungs of the Earth'.
- Every day we lose an area bigger than New York City.

RESEARCH

Choosing a focus

1 Read STUDY SKILL Use the words in the box to complete the table with the topics. Then add a focus for each topic.

> ~~endangered animals~~   green transport   factories and industry
> solar power   air pollution   ~~gorillas~~   green energy
> bicycles

Topic	Focus
endangered animals	gorillas

2 Read STUDY SKILL Look at the diagram showing how a researcher chose a research focus. Write the words on the diagram.

> Which   Where   Topic

| _____ | Endangered animals | → | _____ ? | Africa | → | _____ ? | Gorillas |

Focus: endangered gorillas in Africa

3 Work in pairs. Complete the diagrams with the words in the box. Then write the research focus.

> wind energy   Where?   South America   Which?   steel   Where?

1 | Topic | air pollution | → | _____ ? | cars | → | Where? | _____ |

Focus: _____

2 | Topic | factories and industry | → | Which? | _____ | → | _____ ? | China |

Focus: _____

3 | Topic | green energy | → | _____ ? | Europe | → | Which? | _____ |

Focus: _____

4 Work in pairs. Choose one of the topics in the box below. Then use a diagram and ask questions to choose a focus.

> animals in danger   water   air pollution   climate change

Mountain gorillas

Air pollution from a paper mill

King penguins

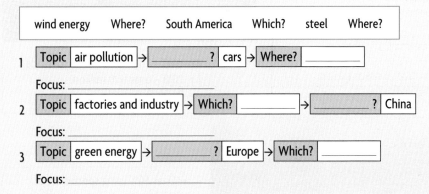
Houses on the edge of an ice cliff

REVIEW

1 Read the introduction to a talk. Circle the key words.

> ### Introduction
>
> Hello everyone. Today's session is the second of our lectures focusing on organizations and the environment. This week we're looking at the World Wide Fund for Nature, the WWF, one of the leading international groups working for the environment. A key area of the WWF's work is in biodiversity. Stop and think for a moment – think of all the different types of plants and animals in the world, the different flowers, trees, animals – this is biodiversity. Biodiversity can be badly affected by humans and the damage we do to the environment.

2 🔊 3.8 Read and listen to the introduction. <u>Underline</u> the words stressed by the speaker. Are they the same as the key words?

3 🔊 3.9 Listen to the WWF's two areas of focus. Write the key words in the table.

protect   key places   animals   plants   important   biodiversity

Key words	Main points
1	
2	

4 Work with a partner. Use the key words to write the two main points in the table above.

5 You are going to listen to more of the talk. Read the questions and write the type of answer for each question.

year   length of time   number

Questions	Type of answer	Answers
How many tourists visit the Mediterranean each year?	number	
How long will it take for a big increase in visitors to happen?		
How long is the European Mediterranean coastline?		
How many projects does the WWF have in the Mediterranean region?		
When did the WWF start?		

6 🔊 3.10 Listen and write the answers to the questions in exercise 5.

7 🔊 3.11 Listen and write down the numbers + nouns.

a   *34 million people*   e _____
b   _____   f _____
c   _____   g _____
d   _____

8 Work with a partner. Say the exact numbers in exercise 7. Then say the numbers not in their exact form using *of*, for example: *millions of people.*

4 Modern architecture

LISTENING SKILLS Listening for reasons • Making listening easier
SPEAKING SKILLS Giving reasons • Presentations (2)
VOCABULARY DEVELOPMENT Words that go together (1) • Linking words • Building your vocabulary

LISTENING Houses in the future

1 Work with a partner. Answer the questions.

1 What were houses in your country like in the past?
2 What are they like now?
3 Do you think buildings will be different in the future? How?

2 🔊 **4.1** Listen to the introduction to a discussion. What are the two experts going to talk about?

3 🔊 **4.1** Listen again and complete the information about the two experts.

Modern apartments in Cambridge, Massachusetts

Name   Professor Abdin

Nationality _____

Job _____

Name   Carla Martinez

Nationality _____

Job _____

4 Here are some of the main points from the discussion. Read the sentences and predict the correct answers.

1 Houses will be **very / slightly** different.
2 Houses will be **more expensive / cheaper** to build.
3 We will need **a few / a lot** more houses.
4 Rooms will be **smaller / bigger**.
5 Houses will get power from the **wind / sun**.

5 🔊 **4.2** Listen and check your answers. Do any of the answers surprise you?

Ancient Roman houses in Herculaneum

6 🔊 4.2 Listen to the discussion again. Write the reason for each main point in the table.

Main point	Reason	Words/expressions
1 Houses will be very different.	*new building materials, growing population, environment*	*because of*
2 Houses will be easier and cheaper to build.		
3 We will need a lot more houses.		
4 Rooms will be smaller.		
5 All buildings will have solar panels.		

7 Read STUDY SKILL 🔊 4.3 Listen to the reasons given in the discussion. Complete the table in exercise 6 with the words and expressions the speakers use to give their reasons.

> **STUDY SKILL** Listening for reasons
>
> Speakers usually give reasons for their main points. They can use:
> - **because**: *The house is expensive because it is big.*
> - **so**: *The house is big, so it is expensive.*
> - **to** + infinitive: *You need electricity to heat the building.*
>
> When taking notes, always make a note of reasons the speaker gives for the main points.

8 Work with a partner. Use your notes from exercise 6 and discuss the main points made by the speakers. Do you agree or disagree?

9 Read STUDY SKILL Work with a partner. Answer the questions.
1 Which of these strategies did you use when you listened to the discussion?
2 Which do you always use?
3 Which do you need to use more?

> **STUDY SKILLS** Making listening easier
>
> In classroom listening activities, you can use strategies to make listening easier.
>
> Before you listen:
> - look at the information on the paper, including pictures.
> - read the questions.
> - try to predict answers.
>
> While you listen:
> - focus. Don't look around.
> - don't worry if you miss an answer. Go on to the next one.
> - use short forms to write answers.

SPEAKING Giving reasons

1 Work with a partner. Look at the pictures of different kinds of campuses. Match some of the words with the pictures.

> old   modern   big   small   hi-tech   out of town
> green   lively   quiet   central

2 Work with a partner. Which of the campuses are similar to your college campus?

3 **Read STUDY SKILL** Work with a partner. What kind of campus do you prefer? Why?

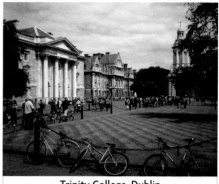

Trinity College, Dublin

> **STUDY SKILL** Giving reasons
>
> When you are discussing things, you need to give reasons for your ideas. Two useful words are:
>
> *because /so*
>
> I prefer an old campus *because* **I like traditional architecture.**
>
> **I like traditional architecture,** *so* I prefer an old campus.
>
> The sentences mean the same thing.

4 Match the sentence parts and add *because* or *so*.

> I love using technology   I need a small campus.
> I like a quiet campus   I don't like a quiet campus.
> I like being close to nature   so   I don't have my own car.
> I get lost very easily   because   I prefer a hi-tech campus.
> I like busy places with lots to do   I don't like too many people around.
> I prefer a central campus   I like a green campus.

University library, Miami, Florida

5 🔊 4.4 Listen and check your answers.

6 🔊 4.5 Listen to the first part of the sentences. Complete the sentences with your own answers.

7 Think about your campus. Write three things you like about your campus, and three possible improvements you would make.

COLLEGE CAMPUS	
Like	Improvements
1	
2	
3	

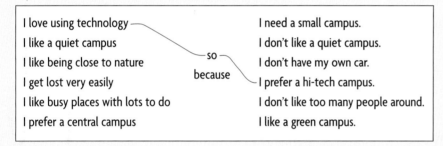

Knowledge Village, Dubai

8 Work with a partner. Discuss what you like about your campus and what improvements you would make. Give reasons.

Planning a campus

9 Your college is planning a new campus. The college wants student ideas on the new design. Put the factors in order of importance for you.

- ☐ the look of the campus
- ☐ the size of the campus
- ☐ the location of the campus
- ☐ the number of outdoor green spaces
- ☐ the number of sports and leisure facilities

10 Work in a group. Compare your answers and discuss your ideas. Give reasons for your ideas.

11 As a group, decide which three factors from exercise 9 are the most important.

12 In your group, plan the new campus and its facilities. Make notes of your ideas and draw your campus plan.

13 Read the expressions in the Language Bank. Work in a group. Prepare to present your plan to the rest of the class.

> **LANGUAGE BANK** Making plans
>
> *We are going to have ...*
> *There is going to be ...*
> *There are going to be ...*
> *There will be ...*
> *We will have ...*

14 **Read STUDY SKILL** Practise presenting the plan to your own group.

> **STUDY SKILL** Presentations (2)
>
> When you talk to a group, you need to:
> - look at your audience.
> - make eye contact.
> - speak clearly.
> - use good body language.

15 Present your plan to the class. Listen to the presentations from the other groups and take notes.

16 Work in a group. Discuss the other presentations. Which is the best campus plan? Who gave the best presentation? Why?

Teaching Block · Library · Accommodation Blocks · Science Laboratories · IT Block

VOCABULARY DEVELOPMENT Building your vocabulary

1 Read STUDY SKILL Match the verbs in the box with the nouns below.

| give | do | get | attend | have |

1 _____ lunch / a break
2 _____ information / a book / a good mark
3 _____ an assignment / some independent study
4 _____ a lecture / a presentation / college
5 _____ a presentation / a summary

2 Read STUDY SKILL Underline the places where the words are linked.

1 attend a presentation
2 give a summary
3 get information
4 have a break
5 eat in the cafeteria
6 research a topic
7 give an answer
8 ask a question

3 4.6 Listen and check your answers. Then listen again and repeat.

4 Read STUDY SKILL Complete the table with some of the verbs and nouns from exercise 1.

Things you do	Where you do them
attend a lecture	in the lecture hall
	from the library
	in a study room
	from the teacher
	in the cafeteria
	in the auditorium
	in class

attend

give

do

get

have

REVIEW

1 Read the main points from a talk about studying architecture. Predict which of these statements are true (T) or false (F).

1 Architecture students are usually the same type of person. ___
2 Some architecture graduates are imaginative, others are practical. ___
3 Architecture students have to be good learners. ___
4 All architecture students work as architects when they graduate. ___
5 You will only get work in the country where you studied. ___

2 ◎ 4.7 Listen and check your answers.

3 ◎ 4.8 Listen to a student talking about which college she goes to and the courses she is taking. <u>Underline</u> the stressed words.

> I'm from China. I study at DTU, the Design and Technology University. I'm studying architecture and my courses include Design, Computer Graphics, Physics, Maths and, of course, English.

4 ◎ 4.9 Listen and choose the reasons she gives for taking these courses.

Courses	Reasons
architecture	love designing buildings / want to get a good job
design, computer graphics, maths, physics	will help me get a good job / I have no choice
English	I need it for my studies and work / I need it for travelling

5 Work with a partner. Compare your answers.

6 Complete the table with the courses you are studying and your reasons for choosing them.

Courses	Reasons

7 Work with a partner. Tell your partner which courses you are taking and why. Use *because* and *so* to talk about your reasons.

5 How we learn

LISTENING SKILLS Listening to new information • Knowing your learning style
SPEAKING SKILLS Disagreeing • Taking turns
VOCABULARY DEVELOPMENT Making language stronger

LISTENING Learning styles

1 Think of five things good learners do. Make notes.

2 Work with a partner. Discuss your notes. Decide on the three most important things that good learners do and write them below. Which ones do you do?

1 _____

2 _____

3 _____

• Good learners review their notes before the next class.
•
•
•
•

3 🔊 **5.1** Listen to the introduction to a talk. Complete the learning styles on the diagram.

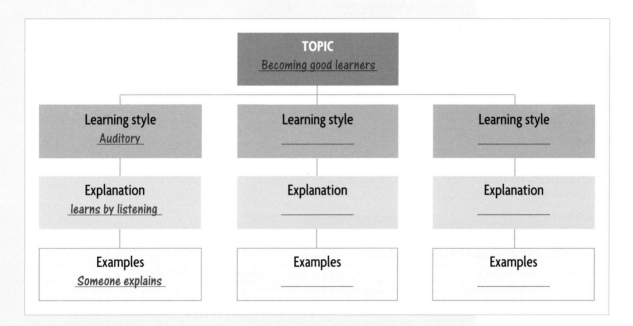

TOPIC
Becoming good learners

Learning style
Auditory

Learning style
_____

Learning style
_____

Explanation
learns by listening

Explanation
_____

Explanation
_____

Examples
Someone explains

Examples
_____

Examples
_____

4 **Read STUDY SKILL** 🔊 **5.2** Listen to the next part of the talk. Add the key words for each explanation to the diagram.

STUDY SKILL Listening to new information

When you listen for new information, you should listen for:
- key words.
- an explanation of the new information.
- examples of the new information.

---

5 🔊 **5.2** Listen again and add an example for each explanation.

6 🔊 5.3 Listen to the sentences and decide if you agree or disagree with each one. Write your answers in the table.   agree = A   disagree = D   not sure = ?

a			b			c		
	Answers	Points		Answers	Points		Answers	Points
1	___	___	5	___	___	9	___	___
2	___	___	6	___	___	10	___	___
3	___	___	7	___	___	11	___	___
4	___	___	8	___	___	12	___	___
TOTAL =			TOTAL =			TOTAL =		

7 🔊 5.4 Listen and find your three scores. Write them in the table.

8 🔊 5.5 Listen and write the names of the learning styles a–c in the table.

9 Work with a partner. Compare and discuss your scores. Do you agree? Think of three ways you can use this information.

10 **Read STUDY SKILL** Work with a partner. Look at the list of learning activities. Which do you think are best for each learning style? Write A (Auditory), V (Visual), or T (Tactile).

Learning activity	Learning style
listening to documentaries	
using diagrams and pictures	
doing practical classes	
taking notes	
going on trips	
using different colour pens	
doing role plays in class	
making models	
recording lectures and notes	
talking in groups	

STUDY SKILL Knowing your learning style

Most people have an individual learning style. Good learners know their own learning style.

Your learning style could be: **auditory visual tactile**

You can do different things to improve your listening in English.
- Visual learners: watch TV documentaries.
- Auditory learners: join an English discussion group to share ideas.
- Tactile learners: join a practical class to learn a new skill.

11 🔊 5.6 Listen and check your answers.

12 Work with a partner. Answer the questions.
1 Which activities in exercise 10 do you enjoy doing?
2 Do your choices match your learning style?
3 What other activities would be good for your learning style?
4 Which activities from today's lesson match your learning style?

SPEAKING Giving opinions

1 Work with a partner. Read the statements. Find two that you both agree with and two that you both disagree with.

'People always dream in colour.'

'Childhood is the best time of your life.'

'School should start when you are four years old.'

'Mobile phones should be banned in restaurants.'

'Winter is better than summer.'

'A good education is more important than money.'

'Family is more important than friends.'

2 5.7 Listen to some people giving their opinions. Tick (✓) the expressions they use.

	I think …	I really think …	In my opinion …	I agree with you.	That's a good point, but …	I really don't agree.
1						
2						
3						

3 Read the statements and decide if you agree or disagree.
1 We learn more by talking about our ideas than if we work alone.
2 The best way to learn about something is to read about it.
3 A good teacher is the most important thing for learning at college.
4 You can only learn if you want to learn.
5 You learn the same way now as you did when you were a child.

4 Read the expressions in the Language Bank. Then work with a partner and discuss your opinions.

LANGUAGE BANK Opinions

Giving your opinion
In my opinion, …   I think …

Giving someone else's opinion
According to …   He/She thinks …

Agreeing
I agree.   That's a very good point.
I completely agree.   You're right.

Disagreeing
I don't agree.   I don't think that is the case.
I don't think so.   That's a good point, but …

---

5 Read STUDY SKILL Read the statements. Write a response disagreeing with each one.

> Everyone should go to college.
> <u>That's a good point, but there aren't enough places for everyone at the moment.</u>

1 All students should study Maths.

_____

2 Group work helps me to learn more than when I work on my own.

_____

3 Colleges should spend money on gyms, not libraries.

_____

STUDY SKILL Disagreeing

It is important to be polite when you disagree.

When you disagree, you should give a reason.

That's a good point, but I think group work is more important.
I don't agree. In my opinion, group work is essential.

---

6 Work with a partner. Say each statement in exercise 5 and listen to your partner's response. Is it the same as yours? Can you continue the discussion?

7 Read STUDY SKILL Match the problems with the pictures a–c.

☐ someone is not speaking enough
☐ someone is speaking too much
☐ someone thinks the other person wasn't polite when they interrupted

---

STUDY SKILL Taking turns

When you work in a group, you should take turns at speaking.

Including people in the discussion
A common problem in group work is when a person doesn't speak enough.
You can help other people speak by using these phrases with their name:

What do you think, Marianne?
What's your opinion, Raoul?

Interrupting someone
Another problem is when a person speaks too much. You can interrupt, but remember to be polite.

Excuse me, …
Can I say something here?

---

8 Can you think of any solutions for each problem in exercise 7? Make notes.

9 Work in a group. Discuss the pictures, the problems, and your notes. Decide on the best solution for each problem.

a

b

c

VOCABULARY DEVELOPMENT   How strong is your opinion?

1   **Read STUDY SKILL** Work with a partner. Read the expressions and answer the questions.

I agree.	I don't think so.	Yes, I suppose so.
I totally disagree.	I'm not sure.	No, I don't agree.
That's exactly how I see it.		

1   Which words show that the person agrees or disagrees?
2   Which expression shows that the person is undecided?
3   Which words make the expressions stronger?

STUDY SKILL   Making language stronger

We can use these expressions to express a strong opinion:

I agree.   *I completely agree.*   *That's exactly how I see it.*
I don't agree.   *I don't agree at all.*   *I totally disagree.*

We can use these expressions to express a less strong opinion:

Yes, I suppose so.
I don't think so.
That's a good point, but …

2   Complete the expressions with the words in the box. You can use some words more than once.

totally	completely	excellent	really	at all	good

	Agree	Disagree
Strong	I _____ agree. I _____ agree. That's an _____ point. I _____ agree with you.	I _____ disagree. I don't agree _____ . I _____ disagree. I _____ don't agree. I _____ don't think so.
Less strong	I agree. That's a _____ point.	I don't think so. I don't agree.

agree

disagree

3   Work in a group. Discuss the statements. Give your opinion, and agree and disagree with other students.
1   The most important thing at college is to pass all your exams.
2   The destruction of rainforests is the most important environmental problem in the world.
3   Childhood is the best time of your life.

REVIEW

1 🔊 5.8 Listen to the start of a lecture about multiple intelligences. Answer the questions.

1 How many different types of intelligence will the lecture be about?
2 Whose theory about multiple intelligences is this?

2 🔊 5.9 Listen to the next part of the lecture. Complete the table with the names of the intelligences.

| mathematical | naturalist | linguistic | musical | interpersonal |

Intelligence	Key ideas from the explanation
1	learn languages / spoken, written language
2	analyze problems / think logically
3 bodily-kinesthetic	
4 spatial	
5	compose, perform music
6	understand other people / work well in groups
7 intrapersonal	
8	recognizing, naming / environment

3 🔊 5.9 Listen again. Complete the table in exercise 2 with the missing key ideas.

4 Write the expressions in the box in the correct place in the table below.

I think …	What's your opinion, Raoul?
I completely agree.	Can I say something here?
In my opinion, …	I'm afraid I don't agree.
That's a very good point.	What do you think, Marianne?
I don't think that is the case.	Excuse me, …

giving your opinion	
agreeing	
disagreeing	
including someone	
interrupting someone	

5 Write two statements about learning.

You learn more when you work in a group.

6 Work in a group. Discuss your statements from exercise 5. Express your opinions, and agree and disagree with other students.

6 Living with technology

LISTENING SKILLS Taking notes (3) • Using criteria
SPEAKING SKILLS Presentations (3) Using a checklist
VOCABULARY DEVELOPMENT Words that go together (2)
RESEARCH Asking research questions

LISTENING Technology improving lives

1 Work with a partner. Answer the questions.

1 What technology have you used today?
2 What did people do before they had this technology?

2 🔊 **6.1** Listen to the description of a simple technology, the bicycle ambulance. Label the diagram using the words in the box.

> patient   trailer   person who pedals   passenger   bicycle

3 You are going to listen to some information about bar codes. Before you listen, think about what happens when you buy things at a supermarket. Work with a partner and put the steps in order.

☐ the cashier scans the items
☐ pay for the items
☐ put the items on the counter
☒ queue up
☐ put the items in bags

1 _____
2 _____
3 _____
4 _____

bicycle ambulance

5 _____

4 🔊 **6.2** Listen to the information about bar codes. What two problems have bar codes solved?

1 ☐ They save time and money.
2 ☐ They help shop assistants to use machines.
3 ☐ They help shop assistants to sell more things.
4 ☐ They allow shops to have fewer shop assistants.

5 **Read STUDY SKILL** 🔊 **6.2** Listen again. Make a note of key words and of any words you don't understand.

bar code

STUDY SKILL Take notes (3)

Sometimes when you are taking notes, you hear new words that you didn't recognize. When you hear new words, use these strategies to help you understand.

- Make a note of the word and any words that go with it (don't worry about spelling).
- Ask yourself these questions:
  Is there an explanation or example in the talk?
  What do I know about the topic?
  Do the visuals help?
- Check the word in the dictionary or ask someone.

6 Work with a partner. Discuss the meaning of the words you wrote in exercise 5. Then check the meanings of the words in a dictionary.

7 You are going to listen to a podcast about the two developments in technology in exercises 2 and 4. Before you listen, predict and complete the table with the information in the box.

> every day / in an emergency
> all over the world / mainly in developing countries
> 20 items = $1 / 1 item = around $100
> cost of maintaining an ambulance / time needed to check prices

hand-held scanner

Information required	Technology 1 – bicycle ambulance	Technology 2 – barcode
When used	in an emergency	every day
Where used		
Cost		
Problem it solves		

8 6.3 Listen to the podcast. Work with a partner. Check your answers.

9 6.3 Listen again. Are the sentences true (T) or false (F)?

1 ☐ Hospitals are often a long way from villages.
2 ☐ Ambulances aren't very expensive.
3 ☐ The bicycle ambulance can carry only the person who is ill.
4 ☐ Bar codes were first used in the 1970s.
5 ☐ Scanners are quite difficult to use.
6 ☐ Bar code technology has an impact on everyone.

10 Work with a partner. Prepare to give a summary of the two developments in technology. Put the parts of your summary in order.

☐ your opinion
☐ description of item
☐ description of problem

11 Work with a partner. Take turns to give a summary of the two technologies.

12 Read STUDY SKILL 6.4 Listen to the last part of the podcast. The speaker is talking about how to choose the best technology. Complete the table with the speaker's criteria and questions.

Criteria	Questions
1 _____ on our lives	Which has had the biggest _____ ?
2 _____ for money	Which is the best _____ ?
3 _____	Which is the most _____ ?

13 Work with a partner. Evaluate the two technologies using the questions in exercise 12.

STUDY SKILL Using criteria

We use criteria to evaluate something.

For example: Which is the best form of transport, car, train, or plane?

Possible criteria:
- speed – *Which is the fastest?*
- environment – *Which is the least damaging?*
- cost – *Which is the best value for money?*

SPEAKING Presenting information

1 Look at the picture of a 21st-century classroom. Label the furniture and equipment in the classroom.

> book shelves   smart board   adjustable chair
> ergonomic desk   laptop   projector

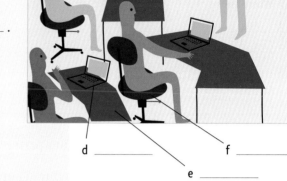

a _____   b _____
c _____

d _____   f _____
e _____

2 Read the expressions in the Language Bank. Look at the picture again. Complete the sentences.

1 At the top there is a _____ .
2 There is a student typing on a _____ in the middle.
3 On the right there are some _____ .
4 There are some students sitting on _____ in the foreground.
5 In the background a teacher is pointing to a _____ .

> **LANGUAGE BANK** Describing a picture
>
> *This picture shows …*
> *… on the left …*   *… at the top …*
> *… on the right …*   *… at the bottom …*
> *… in the foreground …*   *… in the middle …*
> *… in the background …*

3 Check your answers with a partner.

4 Work with a partner. Cover the picture. Describe it to your partner from memory. Then change roles. Who gave the most complete description?

5 **Read STUDY SKILL** Look at the presentation slide. What does it show?

> ### Internet users in the world
> - 1,800 million – 2009
> - 360 million – 2000

> **STUDY SKILL** Presentations (3)
>
> Numbers are very powerful. Use them in presentations to have more impact. To use them well:
> - make numbers simple: *4 million* NOT *3,965,488*.
> - explain the numbers: *20,000 – that's 10%.*
> - compare numbers: *650, that's 50 more than last year.*
> - use only a few important numbers.

6 Read part of a presentation about the Internet. Complete it with the information from the slide.

> 'As you can see, there are many [1]_____ users in the world now. The first figure shows the number of users in 2009 – approximately [2]_____ worldwide. This number is much bigger than the number of users in 2000 – [3]_____ . So according to statistics, the number of Internet users in the world is growing quickly.'

7 🎧 6.5 Listen and check your answers.

8 Read the expressions in the Language Bank. <u>Underline</u> the expressions used in the presentation in exercise 6.

9 Work with a partner. Practise presenting the information on the slide above.

> **LANGUAGE BANK**
> Explaining your numbers
>
> *As you can see …*
> *According to statistics …*
> *The first figure shows …*

Presenting the facts

10 Work in a group. Your topic is 'Technology in the past 50 years'. Choose a focus for your research.

  a Saving people's lives

  b Making people's lives easier

11 In your group, decide which development in technology you will research. Then complete the table below with your information.

TOPIC	Technology in the past 50 years
Focus	
What?	
Who?	
When?	
Why?	
Key numbers and words	
Source	

Early mainframe computer

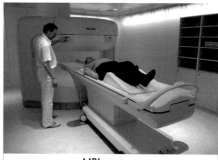

MRI scanner

12 **Read STUDY SKILL** Prepare to explain your group's technology development to the class. Use the checklist in the Study Skill box to help you.

STUDY SKILL Using a checklist

Use a checklist to help you prepare before you give presentation. For example:

Checklist: To do ☑

Prepare	☐ review Language Banks
	☐ make slides or a poster with key words, numbers, and a picture
Practise	☐ learn key words
	☐ say key numbers correctly
	☐ practise aloud

---

13 Present the technology development to the class. Listen to the other groups. Which is the best technology? Who gave the best presentation?

Early mobile phone

VOCABULARY DEVELOPMENT Words that go together

1 **Read STUDY SKILL** Write the words that go with *problem* and *solution*.

| look for | have | a big | find | a major | offer | face |
| a good | the main | solve | an effective | the best | | |

STUDY SKILL Words that go together (2)

Collocations are words that go together. Many verbs, nouns, and adjectives have collocations.

problem	*have a problem*: verb + noun
	a major problem: adjective + noun
solution	*look for a solution*: verb + noun
	a good solution: adjective + noun

When you learn key words, learn their collocations too.

2 Complete the sentences.

1 We need to find a _____ quickly.
2 The main _____ we're facing is the number of people.
3 Together we can solve the _____ .
4 Solar power could be an effective _____ .
5 We must start _____ for a solution.

3 ⊚ 6.6 Listen and check your answers.

RESEARCH Asking research questions

1 **Read STUDY SKILL** Plan some research.

1 Choose an item using technology which is an important part of your life now.
2 Write research questions to find out more about this item.
3 Decide where you are going to research the information.
4 Find the answers to your questions.

STUDY SKILL Asking research questions

Think of questions about your topic focus.

Use question words to help you to think of research questions. For example:

Topic – technology

Research focus – satellite navigation

Who invented it? Why? When?
Who uses it?
What does it do?
What does it replace?
Where is it used?

2 Compare your research questions with a partner. Which were the most useful questions?

Verb

have	
_____	a problem
_____	
_____	
_____	a solution

Adjective

_____	
_____	problem
_____	
_____	
_____	solution

REVIEW

1 🎧 6.7 Listen to three people introducing their talks and make a note of the topics.

Speaker	Topic	Examples
A		
B		
C		

2 🎧 6.7 Listen again and make a note of one example each person gives.

3 🎧 6.8 Listen to part of a talk on worldwide telephone use. Write the title of the slide.

```
◗◖ Worldwide Telephone Use ◗◖

Fixed _____ lines in _____

Europe              _____ %

The Americas        _____ %

Asia & Pacific      _____ %

Arab countries      _____ %

Africa              _____ %
```

4 🎧 6.9 Listen and complete the numbers on the slide.

5 Work with a partner. Practise saying the numbers on the slide. Then practise presenting the information.

6 🎧 6.10 Read and listen to the text. <u>Underline</u> the stressed words and syllables as you listen.

> These bicycle ambulances help solve a common but very serious problem in developing countries. How do you get someone to hospital when they are ill or injured? Hospitals are usually quite far from the remote villages where people live, ambulances are expensive, and there are often no good roads for them.

7 Work with a partner. Practise reading the text aloud.

7 Language and culture

LISTENING Excuse me, do you speak English?

1 Work with a partner. Answer the questions.

  1 How many languages do you speak?

  2 Is more than one language spoken in your country?
    When are the different languages used?

  3 What languages do children learn at school in your country?

2 🔊 7.1 Listen to the opening of a lecture. Complete the information about the lecturer. Tick (✓) the subject she mentions.

Lecturer
Name _____
Job   _____
Research interests
how _____ changes over _____

☐ language learning difficulties
☐ bilingualism
☐ the importance of writing

3 🔊 7.1 Listen again. How many opportunities will there be for questions?

4 **Read STUDY SKILL** 🔊 7.2 Listen to the start of a tutorial following the lecture. How many people are present?

5 🔊 7.2 Listen again. Write the names of the people.

  • the tutor _____

  • the visiting speaker _____

  • the students _____   _____   _____

6 🔊 7.2 Write the relationship between the speakers. using the words in the box Then listen again and check your answers.

classmates   colleagues   friends

a Roxanna, Ronesh, and Simon _____
b Dr Harper and Professor Birchill _____

7 🎧 7.3 Listen to the numbers. Write them down.

1 _____ 4 _____ 7 _____
2 _____ 5 _____ 8 _____
3 _____ 6 _____ 9 _____

8 **Read STUDY SKILL** Look at the table of facts. Predict which numbers from exercise 7 go with each fact below.

Number	Fact
a approximately 75	the percentage of international journal articles written in English
b	the percentage of international science journal articles written in English
c	the estimated number of languages which have died out
d	the number of years ago Latin was still used
e	the number of native and non-native speakers of English worldwide
f	the percentage of the world's population which is bilingual
g	the fraction of the budget for translating at international conferences
h	the number of official languages in the European Union
i	the percentage of Internet content written in English

9 🎧 7.4 Work with a partner. Listen and check your answers.

10 **Read STUDY SKILL** What were the main points in the tutorial? Tick (✓) the main point for each part.

1 ☐ more science articles are written in English than other subjects
☐ to be successful academically you need to learn English

2 ☐ languages die out, but this is natural
☐ Latin was important in the past but is not now

3 ☐ more people will use two languages in the future
☐ people will use their mother tongue less in the future

4 ☐ having one global language helps communication and saves money
☐ many languages are spoken in the European Union

5 ☐ many business people from different countries have meetings face-to-face
☐ English is used for communicating in business and on the Internet

---

STUDY SKILL Deciding on the main points

Lectures and presentations usually make several points. Some of these points will be the main points.
Some languages will die out – this is natural.

Other points support these main points. These supporting points will be examples and facts.
600 years ago all educated people in Europe read and understood Latin, but now where is this language?

There will usually be several supporting points for each main point.

---

11 🎧 7.4 Listen again and check your answers.

12 Work in a group. Discuss each of the main points from the tutorial. Give your opinions and agree and disagree with each other.

STUDY SKILL Taking notes (4)

Numbers are very important for supporting points. You need to:
- note numbers accurately.
- note what the number refers to.

After you take note of facts and numbers, review them. Ask yourself if the number is possible, e.g.
Number of language in the European Union – 223(?)

In your follow-up research, check the accuracy of the numbers.

español

English

SPEAKING Starting your presentation

1 Work with a partner. Discuss which aspects of culture are important for you.

food	family	names	arts	language	literature
festivals	beliefs	customs	sports	clothes	music

2 Work with a partner. Answer the questions.

1 Who do we learn each part of our culture from?
2 What happens to your culture if you go to live in a different country?
3 Which parts of culture change over time and which do not?

3 7.5 Listen and match the students' answers to questions 1–3 in exercise 2. Were any the same as your answers?

a ☐
b ☐
c ☐
d ☐
e ☐
f ☐

4 Think about your culture. Answer the questions.

1 How important is respect for older people?
2 How important is being on time?
3 How important is the written word compared to the spoken?

5 Work in a group. Discuss your answers to the questions in exercise 4.

6 Read the expressions in the Language Bank. Write your opening for a presentation on culture.

7 Work with a partner. Practise the opening to the presentation.

8 🎧 7.6 Listen to the presenter. Is his opening the same as yours?

9 Read STUDY SKILL 🎧 7.6 Listen again and tick (✓) the contractions you hear.

1 I'm ☐
2 I'll ☐
3 I've ☐
4 We'll ☐
5 We're ☐
6 We've ☐

10 You are going to give a presentation on the topic of culture. Write the headings in the outline slide.

My culture	Other cultures	What is culture?

Culture

Outline
- _____
- _____
- _____
- Questions

11 Work with a partner. Write your opening for the presentation.

12 Read STUDY SKILL Work in a group. Give the opening to your presentation. Listen to the other presentations. Use the checklist in the Study Skill box. Tick (✓) the steps that are included. Who gave the best opening?

LANGUAGE BANK Presentation openings

Today I'm going to talk about …
Before I start, I'll give an outline of the presentation.
First, I'll examine …
After that, I'll discuss …
Next, …
Then …
Finally, …
At the end there will be time for questions.

STUDY SKILL Contractions

We often use contractions in presentations:
I'm going to …
We're going to …
I'll …
We'll …

Using contractions makes your English sound natural and fluent.

STUDY SKILL Presentations (4)

The opening of a presentation is the most important part. A good opening gets the audience's attention and tells them what they are going to listen to. When you give a presentation, you might follow these steps:

Checklist
1 Set up your equipment.
2 Stand next to the visual display and face the audience.
3 Welcome the audience, make eye contact and smile.
4 Give the topic of your presentation.
5 Give a short outline of the content.
6 Tell the audience when they can ask questions.

VOCABULARY DEVELOPMENT Synonyms

1 Match the words in the box to the words below with similar meanings.

> difficulty   answer   topic   key   discuss   study   issue
> revise   examine   theme

1 problem   _____ _____
2 learn   _____ _____
3 solution   _____ _____
4 talk about   _____ _____
5 subject   _____ _____

2 **Read STUDY SKILL** Complete the sentences with a synonym of *culture*.
1 Some elements of American and European _____ are the same.
2 The modern _____ is changing quickly.
3 There are many young people in the Urdu-speaking _____ in Britain.

STUDY SKILL Synonyms

A synonym of a word has the same or very similar meaning. For example:

culture   a way of life, beliefs, and customs shared by a group of people: *British culture / modern culture*

Synonyms
society: *Arab society*
community: *the English-speaking community*
world: *the modern world*

Synonyms are useful because they help us to avoid repetition.

---

3 🔊 7.7 Listen and check your answers.

4 Read the opening to the podcast below. Replace the highlighted words in the text with their synonyms in the box. Use the dictionary to help you.

> discuss   topic   society   problems   solutions   study

> Today's podcast is on the [1] subject _____ of multilingualism. This topic is becoming increasingly important in today's [2] world _____ . So the question we will [3] examine _____ today is just what does it mean to live in a multilingual world? To discuss this question, with me today are Dr Hamad and Professor Johnson from Stockton University. They [4] research _____ issues faced by multilingual communities and find [5] answers _____ for particular [6] issues _____ . They recently published a book listing many of their solutions, a book I highly recommend if you want to learn more about multilingualism or you need to study this area for your own research.

5 🔊 7.8 Listen and check your answers.

6 Think about the question below. Think of three ideas to answer the question and write down the key words. Then note down some synonyms for the key words.

   What does it mean to live in a multilingual world?

7 Work with a partner. Discuss your ideas using both the key words and their synonyms.

culture

society

community

world

REVIEW

1 🔊 7.9 Listen and write down the numbers.

a _____ d _____
b _____ e _____
c _____ f _____

2 Look at the table of facts discussed at a tutorial. Predict which number in exercise 1 goes with which fact.

Number	Fact
	Japanese speakers
	consonant sounds in Japanese
	consonant sounds in English
	articles in English
	kanji symbols Japanese children learn
	letters in the English alphabet

3 🔊 7.10 Listen and check your answers.

4 Read the steps to starting a presentation well and number them in the correct order.

- ☐ Tell the audience when they can ask questions.
- ☐ Give a short outline of the content.
- ☐ Welcome the audience, make eye contact and smile.
- ☐ Stand next to the visual display and face the audience.
- ☐ Set up your equipment.
- ☐ Give the topic of your presentation.

5 Work with a partner. From memory, give the steps to starting a presentation well. Use the words in the box below.

> First   Then   Next   After that   Finally

6 Match the synonyms in the box with the four words opposite.

> revise   nation   learn   worldwide
> seminar   state   international
> discussion group

country _____   study _____
       _____   _____
global _____   tutorial _____
       _____   _____

7 🔊 7.11 Read and listen to the opening to a presentation. <u>Underline</u> the verb forms you hear.

8 🔊 7.11 Listen again. Ⓒircle the words the speaker uses to organize her information.

> Today [1] *I'm going to / I'll* talk about language and culture. Before I start, [2] *I'll / we'll* give an outline of the presentation. First, [3] *I'm going to / I'll* talk about the importance of language. After that, [4] *I'm going to / I'll* discuss culture. Finally, [5] *I'll / we'll* look at some examples of the connection between language and culture. In next week's tutorial [6] *I'll / we'll* discuss some of the points in more detail.

9 Work with a partner. Practise saying the opening aloud.

8 Living in the city

LISTENING SKILLS Focusing on organization • Taking notes (5)
SPEAKING SKILLS Pauses • Presentations (5)
RESEARCH Finding sources • Giving references

LISTENING Important cities

1 Which important world cities have you visited? Do you like them? Why?

2 🔊 **8.1** Listen to the first part of a podcast about cities. Number the cities in the order in which they are mentioned.

3 🔊 **8.1** Listen again. What is Brian Davies doing?

- ☐ explaining examples
- ☐ giving an outline
- ☐ answering questions

4 **Read STUDY SKILL** 🔊 **8.1** Listen again. Which three topics will Brian Davies talk about?

- ☐ history   ☐ climate
- ☐ food   ☐ the environment
- ☐ sport   ☐ change
- ☐ recreation   ☐ transport

> ### STUDY SKILL Focusing on organization
>
> Always listen carefully to the introduction to a presentation or talk. It will give you an outline or overview of the content. The introduction will tell you:
>
> - the main topics.
> - how the topics are organized.
>
> This will help you to follow the main part of the talk.

5 Complete the outline for Brian Davies' talk.

Outline
• Topic 1: _____
City: _____
• Topic 2: _____
City: _____
• Topic 3: _____
City: _____

6 🔊 **8.1** Listen again and check your answers.

Rome

Copenhagen

Dubai

7 Which key words and numbers from the main part of the talk do you think are about which city?

> historical   modern   international   10 million visitors
> bicycle   population of 1.7 m   future   green

8 | Read STUDY SKILL | Label the diagrams a–c with the words from the box.

> chart   mind map   timeline

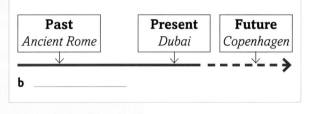

b _____

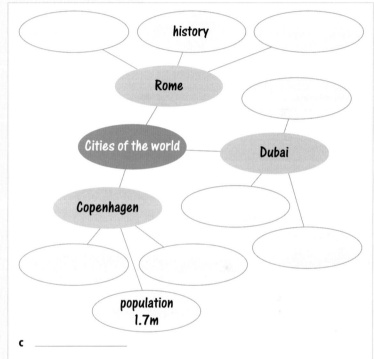

c _____

a _____

STUDY SKILL Taking notes (5)

To learn and remember information more easily, you need good notes. When listening:
- try to get all the main points.
- write the key words clearly.
- be accurate with numbers.
- use mind maps, pictures, and diagrams.

9 Work with a partner. Look at the diagrams. Answer the questions.

1 Which is a good way to take notes of lots of information?
2 Which is a good way to compare numbers?
3 Which is a good way to show time?

10 (◎) 8.2 Listen to the main part of the talk.

1 Complete the mind map in exercise 8.
2 Add more parts to the mind map if necessary.
3 Did you hear any of the words from exercise 7?

11 (◎) 8.3 Listen to three students giving summaries of their notes about the three cities. Tick (✓) the information each student (A–C) includes.

12 Work with a partner. Decide which student gave the best summary and why.

Summary	A	B	C
City name			
Location			
Population			
Best for ...			
Famous building			
Transport			

SPEAKING Comparing cities

1 Work with a partner. Look at the photos of two great cities.

1 What are the two cities?
2 What do you know about these cities?

2 🔊 8.4 Listen to two students discussing the two cities. What is the relationship between the cities?

3 Work with a partner. Discuss the questions.

1 Is your town or city twinned with another town or city?
2 What could be the benefits of a town or city twinning with another place?

4 🔊 8.5 Listen to one student's summary of the two cities and complete the information in the table below.

	Berlin	Istanbul
Approximate population	__ million	__ million
Annual visitors	7.5 million	__ million
Universities		44
Hospitals		
Currency	euro	lira

5 🔊 8.5 Work with a partner. Compare your answers. Then listen again and check.

6 Read the expressions in the Language Bank. Use the expressions and the information in the table in exercise 4 to complete the text.

> **LANGUAGE BANK** Comparing
>
> *If we compare …, we can see that …*
> *A comparison of … shows that …*
> *Istanbul is **far** bigger than Berlin.*
> *Dubai is **slightly** smaller than Copenhagen.*
> *Dubai is almost **as** big **as** Copenhagen.*
> *Rome is **not as** green **as** Copenhagen.*
> ***Both** Copenhagen **and** Dubai are modern cities.*

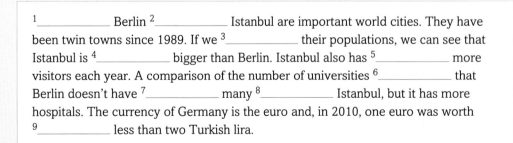

---

¹_____ Berlin ²_____ Istanbul are important world cities. They have been twin towns since 1989. If we ³_____ their populations, we can see that Istanbul is ⁴_____ bigger than Berlin. Istanbul also has ⁵_____ more visitors each year. A comparison of the number of universities ⁶_____ that Berlin doesn't have ⁷_____ many ⁸_____ Istanbul, but it has more hospitals. The currency of Germany is the euro and, in 2010, one euro was worth ⁹_____ less than two Turkish lira.

---

7 🔊 8.6 Listen and check your answers.

8 **Read STUDY SKILL** 🔊 8.6 Listen to the text in exercise 6 again. Mark the pauses with **//**. Work with a partner. Practise reading the text and leaving pauses.

> **STUDY SKILL** Pauses
>
> When we write, we use commas (,) and full stops (.). When we speak, we use pauses to help listeners understand.
>
> Pauses help to:
> - organize our information.
> - emphasize information.
> - show a change of topic.

9 | Read STUDY SKILL | Match steps 1–5 in the Study Skill box with a–e below.

a Istanbul, historically known as <u>Byzantium</u> and <u>Constantinople</u>, is the largest city in <u>Turkey</u> with a population of 13 million. Istanbul is a <u>megacity</u>, as well as the cultural, economic, and financial centre of Turkey.

STUDY SKILL Presentations (5)

Help your audience to understand your information by organizing it well.

1 Choose your topic and focus.
2 Do the research.
3 Make notes on your main points.
4 Write your outline.
5 Organize your information to follow the outline.

☐ **b**
Comparing 2 cities: Berlin and Istanbul

☐ **c**
- population
- history
- geography

☐ **d**
- introduction
- population
  - Berlin
  - Istanbul
- history
  - Berlin
  - Istanbul

☐ **e**
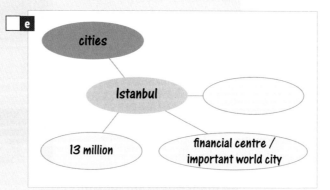

10 Work with a partner. Look at the two presentation outlines below. Answer the questions.

1 How are the outlines the same?
2 How are they different?
3 Which do you prefer? Why?

A

Comparing two cities

- introduction
- Istanbul
  - geography
  - population
  - universities
- Berlin
  - geography
  - population
  - universities

B

Comparing two cities

- introduction
- geography
  - Istanbul
  - Berlin
- population
  - Istanbul
  - Berlin
- universities
  - Istanbul
  - Berlin

11 Work with a partner. Use the information from exercises 4 and 6 to write an introduction to the presentation *Comparing two cities: Istanbul and Berlin.* Then practise saying your introduction.

RESEARCH Information sources

1 | Read STUDY SKILL | Look at the information about a research project. Identify the key words. Then find a suitable website to use for research.

RESEARCH PROJECT	
Topic:	cities
Focus:	future developments
Key Qu.:	What will the next big thing be in cities?
	What problems will it solve?

2 ⊚ **8.7** Listen to three students talking about their research. Write down the key words they use.

Student A	
Student B	
Student C	

3 Use the students' key words and find a good source (a book or website) for each student to use for their research.

4 | Read STUDY SKILL | Choose a type of source in the box below for each title in the table.

| book   website   podcast   TV programme |

Title	Type of source
'Tomorrow's Places', download from www.cities.org	
'Roman Times', Channel 6, BPC	
'The Traveller's Guide to the World' by R. Stone	
www.citiesoflearning.com	

> **STUDY SKILL** Finding sources
>
> Use key words from your topic, focus, and research questions to find information sources. When you use a *search engine* on the Internet, for example, *Google*, type in:
> - only key words.
> - correct spelling.

Internet research

> **STUDY SKILL** Giving references
>
> When you use information, you need to give the source.
>
> **For reading sources**
> - From a **book**: Stone, R. (2004) *The Traveller's Guide to the World*. London, Open Press.
> - From a **website**: Doyle, C. (2009) *Paris, a place to learn*. Retrieved 25th September, 2011, from http://www.citiesoflearning.com
>
> **For listening sources**
> - From a **broadcast** (TV, radio): Simons, A. (Reporter). (7th October, 2010). *Roman Times*, Channel 6, BPC
> - From a **podcast**: Johns, D. (2011) *Tomorrow's Places* (Audio podcast). Retrieved 30th May, 2011, from http://www.cities.org/podcasts

5 Work with a partner. Choose a city and decide on three things you want to know about it.

6 Find the information and give your sources correctly.

REVIEW

1 8.8 Listen to a student giving a summary of a presentation. Complete the outline for the presentation.

Sport and cities
• City 1 _London_
Sport _____
• City 2 _____
Sport _football_
• City 3 _____
Sport _____

2 Look at the research table. Find the missing facts on the Internet and complete the table with the facts and references.

City	Population	Reference
Johannesburg		
Toronto		

3 Find the sources described in the table. Add the references to the table.

Description of source	Reference
a podcast about a capital city	
a book about a country	

4 8.9 Listen and complete the text.

I am going to compare Moscow and Mexico City. [1]_____ Moscow [2]_____ Mexico City are very interesting cities to visit. Mexico City is in South America, [3]_____ Moscow is in Europe. Both Mexico City [4]_____ Moscow are capital cities, but the population of Moscow is not [5]_____ big [6]_____ the population of Mexico City. Mexico City is [7]_____ as cold as Moscow; in fact, the average [8]_____ temperature in Mexico is as high as the average [9]_____ temperature in Moscow.

5 8.9 Listen again and mark the pauses.

6 Practise reading the text aloud.

9 Improving your memory

LISTENING SKILLS Reviewing • Taking notes (6) and (7)
SPEAKING SKILLS Presentations (6) and (7)
VOCABULARY DEVELOPMENT Word families • Knowing vocabulary well

LISTENING Memory

1 Work with a partner. Compare and discuss the meanings of these words.

> learn   memory   revise   remember   memorize

2 Look at the scale. How good are you at remembering these things? Write a number (1–10) for each one.

faces   ☐
numbers   ☐
facts   ☐
names   ☐

Very poor
1
2
3
4
5
6
7
8
9
10
Excellent

3 Compare your answers with a partner.

4 🔊 9.1 Listen to the start of a lecture about memory. Tick (✓) the sentence that best describes the lecturer's opinion.

Students should be active in lectures.   ☐
Students should listen and develop their brains.   ☐
Students should improve their memories.   ☐

5 🔊 9.1 Listen again. Complete the three key questions that the lecture will address.

> 1 How are _____ and _____ connected?
>
> 2 What _____ of _____ are there?
>
> 3 How can we _____ our _____ ?

6 Work with a partner. Discuss the questions in exercise 5.

7 **Read STUDY SKILL** 🔊 9.2 Listen to the next part of the lecture. Tick (✓) the three things the lecturer says about reviewing.

☐ It is a key factor for remembering information.
☐ It was the subject of last week's lecture.
☐ The students will now review last week's lecture.
☐ Today's lecture will include more about reviewing later.

8 🔊 9.3 Listen to the facts about the brain. What do these numbers relate to? Make notes as you listen.

2 _____	100 billion _____	2% _____	20% _____

9 Make brief notes to review what you have learned. Then compare with a partner.

10 🔊 **9.4** Listen to the next part of the lecture. Write down the key words.

11 🔊 **9.5** Listen to the next part of the lecture. Which types of memory does the lecturer say she will talk about today?

☐ working   ☐ sensory   ☐ short-term   ☐ long-term

12 **Read STUDY SKILL** 🔊 **9.6** Listen to the next part of the lecture. Complete the mind map with the uses of each type of memory.

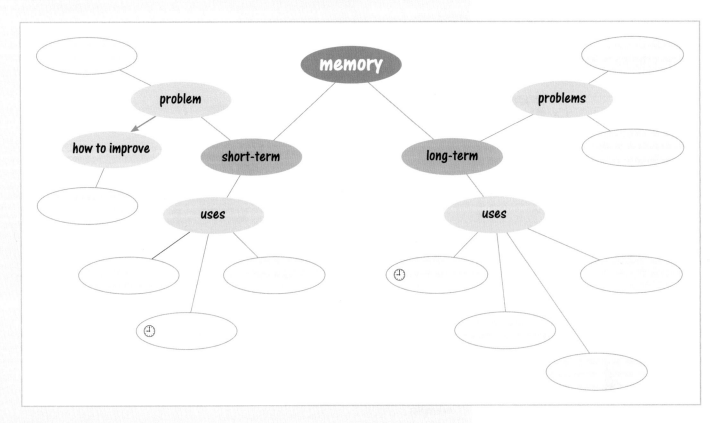

13 🔊 **9.7** You are going to do a task to test your short-term memory. Listen and do the task.

14 🔊 **9.8** Listen to the next part of the lecture about problems with memory, and how to improve your memory. Add notes to your mind map. Then work with a partner to compare and complete your notes.

15 🔊 **9.9** Listen to the next part about reviewing. Why is reviewing important?

16 🔊 **9.10** Listen and complete the advice for taking good notes.

1 You need good notes to be able to _____ effectively.
2 Taking notes helps us to _____ the information later.
3 Write down _____ _____ .
4 Organize the information in _____ _____ .
5 Use _____ prompts, e.g. colours and highlights.
6 Don't use only words; use _____ and _____ .

17 **Read STUDY SKILL** Work with a partner. Compare and complete your notes from the lecture. Check facts if necessary, and reorganize your notes.

18 Use your notes to give a summary of the information from the lecture.

SPEAKING Improving your presentation delivery

1 Match the five senses with the pictures.

- ☐ taste
- ☐ touch
- ☐ sight
- ☐ smell
- ☐ hearing

2 Work with a partner. Discuss the questions.

1 Which sense is most important to you?

2 Which senses do you use the most when you remember things?

3 Read the notes about someone who had a special ability. Complete the notes using the words in the box.

date
profession
results of study
reference
medical study
nationality
special ability
~~name~~
examples of ability

Case study	
1 name	'S'
2	Russian
3	newspaper reporter
4	early 20th century
5	could remember everything
6	– remembered using all five senses – invented stories in pictures to remember – example: 'saw' one sound as a brown line on a dark background, with red sides, tasting of soup
7	studied by a psychologist for 30 years
8	– proved he had memory for everything since he was a baby – did same tests years later – everything still correct – found some problems with memory **example:** – difficulty remembering faces
9	Russell, P. (1986). *The Brain Book*, London, Routledge

4 **Read STUDY SKILL** Read the script for the beginning of a presentation about 'S'. There are no full stops or commas. Complete the tasks below.

> Today's presentations are all about extraordinary people there are many people who are good at things for example maths or music but some people are so good that they seem to be almost incredible I'm going to talk about a famous case of a person with an extraordinary memory I'm going to talk about 'S' first I'll give you the background to his life then I'll describe his condition and give some examples of the things he could do.

1 Add punctuation.

2 Underline the key words and mark their stress.

3 Find and mark the links between words.

4 Mark where you think the pauses are.

5 🔊 9.11 Listen and check.

STUDY SKILL Presentations (6)

To improve your presentation, prepare your script before you practise.

On your script, mark:

- key words and their stress.
- linking sounds.
- pauses.

Example:

He has an excellent memory. // After …

6 🔘 9.11 Read the expressions in the Language Bank. Read and listen to the beginning of the presentation in exercise 4 again. Underline the expressions from the Language Bank that you hear.

7 Work with a partner. Practise reading the script in exercise 4.

8 Work with a partner. Look at the next part of the script. Put the sentences in the correct order.

> ☐ People at work started to notice him because of his memory.
>
> ☐ He also invented stories to remember things.
>
> ☐ 'S' was a Russian newspaper reporter, living in the first part of the 20th century.
>
> ☐ He did this by using all five of his senses: sight, hearing, taste, smell, and touch.
>
> ☐ To give an example, once when he heard a sound, he described it as a brown line on a dark background, with red sides, tasting of soup.
>
> ☐ For example, when the editor of the newspaper talked to the reporters, 'S' never took notes. He remembered everything.

9 🔘 9.12 Listen and check your answers.

10 Work with a partner. Mark the sentences with key words, stress, linking, and pauses. Then practise reading the script.

11 Work with a partner. Write the final part of the presentation script. Use facts from parts 7 and 8 of the table in exercise 3.

12 With your partner, mark the script for stress, linking and pauses. Then practise saying it.

Presenting a case study

13 Work with a partner. Follow these steps.
1 Make a mind map of the types of extraordinary skills people have.
2 Choose the focus for your presentation from this mind map.
3 Research a person with a skill in your focus area. Find key facts about them.
4 Write a presentation script including an introduction.

14 Look at your finished presentation script. Mark the script for stress, linking, and pauses. Practise saying it.

15 **Read STUDY SKILL** Work with a partner and practise your presentation again. Can you make it shorter but also clearer?

LANGUAGE BANK Examples

Giving examples

*I'm going to talk about **a famous case**.*

***To give an example**, he never took notes.*

*He was very special. **For example**, he could remember lists from 20 years ago.*

*He did have some problems with memory. **For instance**, he couldn't remember faces well.*

STUDY SKILL Presentations (7)

To help your audience, you need a good pace when you give your presentation. Remember:

- too slow can be boring
- too fast is difficult to understand

It is best to vary your pace. Slow down for the most important information.

VOCABULARY DEVELOPMENT Word families

1 **Read STUDY SKILL** Complete the sentences with the words from the Study Skill box.

1 Many people in the UK are out of work and looking for _____ .
2 Most companies like _____ qualified people.
3 She is _____ , but she is looking for a job.
4 The company is a very good _____ ; people like working there.
5 He has been an _____ of the university for several years, first as a researcher, now as a lecturer.

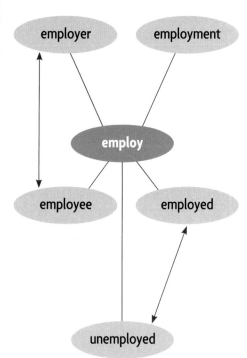

> **STUDY SKILL** Word families
>
> Many words are part of a *word family*, for example:
>
> | | |
> |---|---|
> | *to employ* | verb |
> | *employment* | noun |
> | *employer / employee* | noun (person) |
> | *employed / unemployed* | adjective |
>
> It is a good idea to learn words in a family at the same time.

2 Use your dictionary and complete the other columns for each word.

Verb	Noun	Noun (person)	Adjective
1	memory		
2 to learn			
3	presentation		
4	studies		
5		researcher	

3 Complete the sentences with words from the table.

1 He worked hard to _____ the information.
2 The _____ in this class have very good study skills.
3 My _____ is mainly about short-term memory.
4 You should _____ in a quiet place so that you can focus.
5 I worked on the team for two years as a _____ .

4 **Read STUDY SKILL** Write down the words your teacher says. Write more words in their word families. Then write sentences using the words.

> **STUDY SKILL** Knowing vocabulary well
>
> You need to know vocabulary in different ways. You need to be able to:
> - read, recognize, and understand it instantly.
> - listen, recognize, and understand it instantly.
> - write, use, and spell it correctly and automatically.
> - say, use, and pronounce it correctly and automatically.
> - know other words in the word family.

REVIEW

1 🎧 9.13 Listen to part of a lecture. Which diagram do you think is correct?

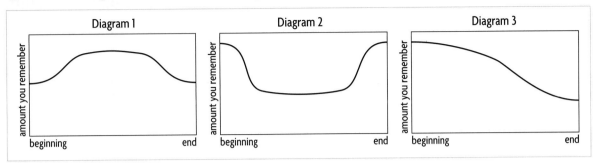

2 🎧 9.14 Listen and check your answer.

3 🎧 9.15 Listen and write the words.

1 _____	4 _____	7 _____
2 _____	5 _____	8 _____
3 _____	6 _____	

4 Work with a partner. You say a word from exercise 3, and your partner says another word from the same word family. Change roles and practise more.

5 Complete the text below with the expressions in the box. You will need to use some expressions more than once.

the case   for instance   example   give an example

For my experiment about learning, I studied two students. In ¹ _the case_____ of the first student, I found that he can remember faces very well. To ² _____ , after seeing someone for only a few seconds, he could recognize them easily from a picture. The second student is an ³ _____ of a person who can't remember faces, but can remember numbers – ⁴ _____ , he can remember all the telephone numbers of his friends. Another ⁵ _____ of his amazing memory is that he can remember fifteen numbers in a row, ⁶ _____ 328957369238276.

6 🎧 9.16 Listen and check your answers.

7 🎧 9.17 Read and listen to the text below. Complete the tasks, then listen again and check.

I will start by asking 'what is the aim of memorization?' then I will look at three key factors that can help anyone memorize information better you should take notes on the worksheet and I will ask you to do some exercises please follow my instructions carefully at the end you can ask questions and then we will have group discussions.

1 Add punctuation to the text.
2 Underline the key words and mark their stress.
3 Find and mark the links between words.
4 Mark the pauses.
5 Practise saying it aloud.

10 Staying healthy

LISTENING   Life begins at 40

1   Work with a partner. Discuss the questions.

1   *Life begins at 40.* What do you think this expression means? Do you agree?
2   Is work more important for younger people or older people?
3   How do people of different ages benefit from exercise?
4   What can older people offer society?

2   🔘 10.1 Listen to the introduction to a podcast about health and age. The presenter is introducing the three speakers. Match the speakers with the topics they will talk about.

1   Dr Hornsey   a   learning and age
2   Elisabeth Lodge   b   health and age
3   Professor Martin   c   older people and work

3   **Read STUDY SKILL** Which types of listening did you use when you listened to the introduction?

4   You are going to listen to Dr Hornsey (speaker 1) talking about health and age. Before you listen, read the last part of her introduction and predict where the numbers go in the text.

Footballers

Flying instructor

| 300 | 39,000 | 1960 | 6,000 | 100 | 61% | 2011 | 65 | 2032 |

… In Britain in ^{1}_____ there were fewer than ^{2}_____ people aged ^{3}_____ or more, but now, in ^{4}_____ , there are about ^{5}_____ , and in 2036 there will probably be ^{6}_____ . By ^{7}_____ it is predicted that there will be a ^{8}_____ increase in the number of people over the age of ^{9}_____ in the UK.

5   🔘 10.2 Listen and complete the text with the numbers. Which strategy did you use for this task?

6   Next, Dr Hornsey talks about four key things we can do to stay healthy all our lives. You are going to write down the four things. Which strategies will you use?

7   🔘 10.3 Listen and write down the four key things Dr Hornsey mentions.

Staying Healthy
1
2
3
4

STUDY SKILL
Reviewing strategies

In this course you have practised many strategies to improve your listening, including:

- predicting
- listening for gist
- listening for specific information
- taking notes effectively
- listening for the main points and examples
- understanding new vocabulary
- deciding who is speaking and the relationship between the speakers

To become an *active listener*, decide which strategies to use when you listen.

8 Dr Hornsey includes more numbers in her talk. Look at the facts and predict the number for each fact.

| 81 | fewer than 20% | 15 billion | 2,200 | 5 | in their 70s and 80s | 2,550 | 1 |

Fact	Prediction	Actual number
number of calories a teenage boy needs daily		
number of calories a man needs daily		
number of portions of fruit and vegetables older people should eat daily		
average age people live to in Japan		
ages at which people still exercise in Japan		
percentage of people in the UK over 65 who get the right amount of exercise		
number of cigarettes sold worldwide daily		
number of medical check-ups you should have every year		

9 🔊 10.4 Decide which strategy you will use when you listen. Then listen and write the actual numbers. How many of your predictions were correct?

10 🔊 10.5 Next, Elisabeth Lodge (speaker 2) discusses her research. You are going to listen and complete her key ideas. Decide which strategy you will use. Then listen and complete the ideas.

people over 65
official retirement age
people who stay in work
stay in work because
teacher of 68

11 🔊 10.6 Professor Clayton Martin (speaker 3) talks about the brain, age, and learning. Listen and write one example that he gives for each main point.

Main point	Example
untrue things people believe about the brain and age	our memory gets worse as we age
good activities for the brain	
famous people who worked till they were old	
careers which people change to when they are 50	

12 Check the spelling and meaning of any new words in your answers to exercise 11.

13 Look at the sentences from the three conclusions given by the speakers. Match the conclusions with the speakers.

1 Dr Hornsey   a   Life is for learning.
2 Elisabeth Lodge   b   Older people have an important role in our community.
3 Professor Martin   c   Don't leave it too late.

14 🔊 10.7 Listen and check your answers.

A painting by Pablo Picasso

SPEAKING Giving a conclusion

1 Work with a partner. Use a dictionary to check the meanings of the words in the box.

> breakthrough discover treat germ surgery cancer antiseptic antibiotic

2 Work with a partner. Answer the questions.

1 What were some of the important medical discoveries in history? Why were they important?

2 Do you know of any famous doctors or scientists who worked in medicine? What did they do?

Abu Bakr Mohammed
Ibn Zakariya al-Razi
(Rhazes) Rhazes

Li Shi-Zhen

Florence Nightingale

Marie Curie

Alexander Fleming

3 Read the notes about some famous people in the history of medicine. Discuss your ideas with a partner. Who do you think was most important? Why?

Person	Dates	Achievement
Abu Bakr Mohammad Ibn Zakariya al-Razi (Rhazes) Rhazes	c 865–925	wrote an encyclopaedia of medicine, 'Al Tasrif', used for 500 years; discovered the difference between smallpox and measles; wrote articles on allergies and fever
Li Shi-Zhen	1518–1593	wrote the most important book in traditional Chinese medicine, including research on botany, zoology, and mineralogy
Florence Nightingale	1820–1910	changed the role of nursing, transformed it into a profession
Marie Curie	1867–1934	discovered radium (used for treating cancer)
Alexander Fleming	1881–1955	discovered the first antibiotic, penicillin, to fight infections

4 Read the Rule. Work with a partner. Cover the information in exercise 3. Ask questions to check the names of the famous people and what they did.

> **RULE** Questions
>
> **Subject**
> - **Who** changed the role of nursing? **Florence Nightingale**.
>   - no auxiliary
>   - word order is the same as the answer
>   - the answer is the subject of the sentence
>
> **Object**
> - **What** did Florence Nightingale change? The **role of nursing**.
>   - auxiliary (*do/does/did*) + base form
>   - question word order changes
>   - the answer is the object of the sentence

5 🔊 **10.8** Read the expressions in the Language Bank. Listen to the conclusion to a presentation. Tick (✓) the phrases in the Language Bank you hear. Which person is the conclusion about?

LANGUAGE BANK Conclusions

Giving a conclusion

To sum up,	*I think that this shows …*
In conclusion,	*I think we can see that …*
Thanks for listening.	*Does anyone have any questions?*
Thank you for listening.	*I am happy to answer any questions.*

---

6 Work with a partner. Choose another person from exercise 3 and write a short conclusion. Then practise giving your conclusion.

7 **Read STUDY SKILL** Read the conclusion below. Match the <u>underlined</u> parts 1–4 with points a–e in the Study Skill box. Which points are not included?

In conclusion, [1]<u>this woman is one of the most important people in the history of medicine</u> for the two reasons presented here. First, [2]<u>she completely changed the role of nurses</u>. Secondly, she worked hard in very difficult places. I think we can see that she is a true role model. [3]<u>Thank you for listening</u>. We have five more minutes so [4]<u>I am happy to answer any questions</u>.

STUDY SKILL Presentations (8)

The end of a presentation should be as strong as the introduction and the main part. In your conclusion you should:

a   remind people of your main points.
b   give your opinion, or recommendation.
c   thank the audience for listening.
d   take questions.
e   maybe include a memorable phrase, e.g. *'Remember, life is for learning!'*

Do not add in new points in your conclusion.

---

8 Work with a partner. Practise giving the conclusion in exercise 7.

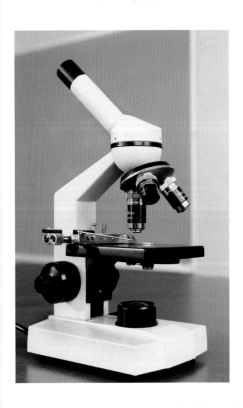

VOCABULARY DEVELOPMENT Describing objects

1 [Read STUDY SKILL] Put the words in the box into the correct column of the table. Add more words.

wood	expensive	paper	square	material	short	plastic	big	cheap
medium-sized	dark	black	metal	blue	long	small	round	light

Made of ...	Shape	Colour	Size	Price

STUDY SKILL Describing things

It is hard to speak if you don't know the vocabulary for objects you want to talk about. However, you don't have to stop speaking. Use other ways of describing the thing you want to talk about.

- It's like a ..., but bigger.
- It's made of ...
- You use it for ... + ing.
- It's [shape/colour/size/price].

2 (🔊) 10.9 Listen to six people describing objects a–f. Which object is each person describing?

1 _____   4 _____

2 _____   5 _____

3 _____   6 _____

3 Work with a partner. Describe the pictures to each other. Which one is your partner describing?

4 Work with a partner. Take turns to choose an object you can see and describe it. Listen and guess what your partner is describing.

RESEARCH Bringing it all together

1 [Read STUDY SKILL] You are going to give a full presentation on an important person from the history of medicine. Follow the steps in the Study Skills box to complete your presentation. Tick (✓) when you finish each part.

2 Work in groups. Give your presentation. While you listen to the other presentations, make notes of facts and also note down your opinion. Use a mind map, bullet points, or a table to focus your notes.

3 Review your notes on all the presentations. Decide who you think is the most important person in the history of medicine.

4 Work in a group. Discuss which person is the most important, and then vote on it.

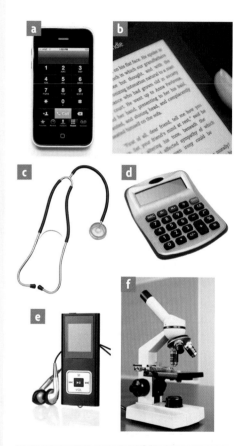

STUDY SKILL
Bringing it all together

Follow these steps to plan and prepare a presentation:

1 choose your research focus.

2 decide on two main points.

3 prepare and organize the body of the presentation.

4 plan an introduction introducing the two main points.

5 plan a conclusion.

6 practise the presentation.

REVIEW

1 Complete the table with the words in the box.

treatment	treated	untreated	to treat
to injure	injured	uninjured	injury
to diagnose	diagnosed	diagnosis	undiagnosed
a bandage	to bandage	bandaged	
hospital	to hospitalize		

Verb	Noun	Adjective

2 Work with a partner. Choose a word from the table in exercise 1. Describe it and ask your partner to guess the word. Then change roles.

3 10.10 Read the answers to some questions. Then listen to the subject and object questions. Circle the part of each sentence that is the answer to the question.

1 Marie Curie discovered radium.
2 Fleming discovered the first antibiotic.
3 Li Shi-Zhen wrote the most important book in traditional Chinese medicine.
4 Florence Nightingale changed the role of nurses.
5 Rhazes wrote an encyclopaedia of medicine.

4 Read a conclusion about life expectancy for children born today. Complete the conclusion using four of the expressions in the box.

Does anyone have any questions?	Thank you for listening.
I am happy to answer any questions.	Thanks for listening.
I think we can see that …	To sum up,
I think that this shows …	In conclusion,

¹_____ people are living much longer nowadays. ²_____ children born today will probably live happy, healthy lives past the age of 100. ³_____ . We have five minutes left so ⁴_____ .

5 Work with a partner. Practise saying the conclusion.

60   **70**   80   90   100

AUDIO SCRIPTS

UNIT 1

1.1

1 Right, everyone, open your books at page 28 – no, sorry, 38.

2 You have 15 minutes to complete the exercise and then we'll go through the answers.

3 Working with the person sitting next to you, read the text about the invention of computers and answer the questions. If you have any problems, put your hand up.

1.2

AO = Admin officer   S = Student

AO Hello. How can I help you?

S I'm a new student here. I'd like some information, please.

AO What do you need to know?

S Well, my name's Laila Suhail and I need to know my student identification number.

AO Laila Suhail, Suhail … yes, here it is. SC8831219.

S Can you repeat that, please?

AO Certainly. SC-883-12-19. Anything else?

S Yes. Can you tell me the room I should go to? I'm doing Computer Studies.

AO You need to go to room F24.

S Sorry, did you say F24?

AO Yes, it's F24.

S Thank you. There's just one more thing. Can you tell me the computer studies course code, please?

AO Yes, it's Infotech 304.

S Can you spell that for me?

AO I-N-F-O-T-E-C-H-three – zero – four.

S Thanks!

1.3

1 Right, I have some announcements to make, so listen carefully. The college bookshop is now open, so you need to go there to collect your books. It's closed all day tomorrow, so I suggest you go today, before 6p.m. Don't forget to take your book list.

2 Next, the college needs to have your mobile phone number, so all students need to give it to their department secretary. Please do that today if possible – we may need to contact you about changes to the timetable.

3 Finally, don't forget there are two lectures this afternoon. Dr Lewis will talk about how college life is different from school life and I will give a talk about how to use the new computer programme that we've put in the library. Both of them start at three. You can choose which one you come to. Both lectures will be repeated on Wednesday.

1.4

1 Hello, I'm Dr Lewis. I hope you're enjoying your first week at college. I'm going to talk about the student contract and what we expect from you at college. You know, college is very different from school. Here at college, we expect a lot more from you.

2 Firstly, at school you had homework, but at college we expect you to work on your own, to work independently. That means you need to learn how to use the library. We expect you to read books, check information using the internet, ask questions, and find out the answers yourself.

3 Another difference is we expect high-quality work from you. We want you to show us that you are a serious student, that you really care about your work. We expect you to work hard at all times, not just enough to pass your exams.

4 Finally, here at college, you are an adult, and we treat you as an adult. You are not school pupils any more. We expect you to be really interested in your subject, to behave well, and to arrive on time for lectures. We also expect you to hand in your work on time.

1.5

1 **A** What's your English teacher's name?
   B Mr Price.

2 **A** Which room is the English class in?
   B It's in room D4.

3 **A** Could you tell me where the cafeteria is?
   B It's next to the library.

4 **A** What's your ID number?
   B It's HS 45772.

1.6

AO = Admin officer   S = Student

S Good morning. Can you give me some information, please?

AO Good morning! Yes, of course. What would you like to know?

S Well, first of all, what's my ID number? My name is Maria Sanchez Gonzalez.

AO Let me see … It's HS 45772. I think you should write it down.

S OK, HS 45773. Is that right?

AO No, it's not 773, it's 772.

S Oh, thanks … and which room is the English class in?

AO Let me check … here it is … it's in room D4.

S Sorry, did you say 'D4'?

AO Yes, that's right. Anything else?

S Yes, please. What's my English teacher's name?

AO It's Mr Price.

S Can you spell that, please?

AO Yes, it's P – R – I – C – E.

S Sorry, can you repeat that, please?

AO P – R – I – C – E.

S Thanks, and one last thing. Could you tell me where the cafeteria is?

AO Next to the library.

S Thank you very much for your help.

AO Not at all. Have a nice day!

1.7

1 Can you spell that, please?

2 Can you repeat that, please?

3 Can you say that again, please?

4 Did you say 'three'?

5 Is this right?

6 Yes, that's right.

7 No, it's 'seven' not 'eight'.

8 No, that's not right.

9 I'm afraid that's wrong.

1.8

a b c d e f g h i j k l m n o p q r s t u v w x y z

1.9

AO = Admin officer   S = Student

AO Please take note of this information, everyone. The teacher for Business 151 is Ms Davidson. That's D – A – V – I – D – S – O – N.

S1 Excuse me – can you repeat that, please?

AO Yes, of course. D – A – V – I – D – S – O – N. Now, the Maths course, Maths 177, is taught by two teachers, Mr Monaghan and Mrs Roberts.

S2 Can you spell the first one, please?

AO Yes, it's M – O – N – A – G – H – A – N.

S1 Did you say J – H – A – N?

AO No, it's G not J. And Mrs Roberts.

S3 Is that R – O – B – E – R – T – S?

AO Yes, that's right. So … where are we, Business, Maths … OK. Lastly, the teacher for English 163 is Miss Taylor. That's T – A – Y – L – O – R.

S2 Can you say that again, please?

AO Yes, it's T – A – Y – L – O – R.

1.10

a I'd like you to work with a partner now. Look at the statements on page 32 and discuss your opinions. In five minutes time, I will ask some of you to report back to the class.

b You've done a great job on researching and presenting your ideas here. I can see you've worked well as a group and that you shared the tasks well. For next time, it would be a good idea to collect all your references together at the end.

c It's very easy to register for courses. Fill in this form and bring it back completed to this desk anytime, along with two photos. We can then give you your student ID card.

d Here's the reference section – we have some excellent books here in the library for project work. You can't borrow these, but you can take them into the research rooms over there – many students find these useful for group-based projects. You can discuss and plan your project there, and ask me for help if you need it.

1.11

AO = Admin officer   S = Student

AO Hi. Can I help you?

S Yes, I'm a 1st Year student here and I'd like to register for the summer courses. My tutor told me to come here to Admin to do this.

AO OK. Well, to register for the summer courses you need to complete this form. We can go through it together. Can you give me your name, please?

S Sarah Marley.

AO Is that S A R A H or without the H?

S With the H.

AO What's your date of birth?

S The ninth of March, 1992.

AO And are you studying full-time or part-time at present?

S I'm a part-time student.

AO Do you know your ID number?

S Yes, it's ST 69001.

AO Can you repeat that, please?

S Yes, it's ST 69001.

AO Thanks. Do you know your course codes?

S Yes, Maths is MAT 8872.

AO M – A – T – 8 – 7 – 7 – 2.

S No, that's not right. It's 8 – 8 – 7 – 2.

AO Sorry, MAT 8872. And your English code?

S LAN 3778.

AO L – A – N – 3 – 7 – 7 – 8. Is that right?

S Yes, that's correct.

AO OK, I just need a couple of contact details. Is your email address the college one?

S Yes, that's right – smarley@citycollege.ac.

AO What's your mobile number?

S 07813 425 561.

AO Could you repeat that, please?

S Yes, it's 07813 425 561.

AO OK, that's all I need. You'll get an email in couple of days.

UNIT 2

2.1

Good morning everyone, and welcome to this seminar. I'm Jenny Porter. I'm your tutor for the Business course. I think I remember all six of you from the interviews … Kaoru, Ahmed, Arzu, David, Jane … right? Maha's starting tomorrow. Now, in a seminar the idea is that we discuss things together – don't be shy, speak up! I want everyone to feel comfortable and relaxed.

2.2

K = Kaoru   T = Tutor   A = Ahmed   D = David

K I have a question. How are we assessed? Is it all exams?

T No, Kaoru, there are many different ways that we assess you … assignments, tests, projects, essays, and exams too, so it's continuous assessment.

K OK, thank you

A When do we do independent work? Don't we have classes or lectures most of the time?

T No, Ahmed, you only have ten hours of lectures every week, and one seminar every week. The rest of the time you can do independent work.

D Erm, when do we have free time? Will we be working all the time?

T No, don't worry, David, it's not all work! You need to learn time management. This means planning your time well so you can do all your work and have some time off.

D Thank you.

2.3

T = Tutor   D = David   AR = Arzu   A = Ahmed

T Any more questions?

D Yes. Do we have to buy any books?

T Yes, you have to buy some business textbooks – I'll give you a list in a minute. Yes, Arzu?

AR Who do I ask if I need help with my independent work?

T When you're studying, you can help each other, and you can ask the librarian for help with research. You can also speak to me every week in the seminar.

A When we work in a group, can we choose who we work with?

T Yes, sometimes you can choose. But we also expect you to work with different people, just like in the real business world. OK, now here is your book list …

2.4

1 When do we start the project?

2 What time do we come to class?

3 How often do we have exams?

4 Where do we get our grades?

2.5

M = Maha   L = Kaoru

M So, what did Jenny say?

K She talked about the business course. There are many kinds of assessments such as projects and assignments, and we have them all through the course … we should check the college website to find out what we have to do. We have ten lectures and a seminar every week – the rest of the time we work independently. We need to plan our time so that we can do everything and still have some free time … – she called it 'time management' – oh, and we need to buy some books – here's the booklist.

M Thanks Kaoru, that's very helpful.

2.6

1 How often do you have lectures?

2 When do you do independent work?

3 What do you do every day?

4 Where do you do independent work?

5 Where do you have tutorials?

2.7

1 Where do you study?

2 Do you get up early?

3 What do you study?

4 Do you go to the gym?

5 When do you go to the gym?

6 Do you study at night?

2.8

Hi everyone. I think we're ready to start. My name is Mark. Let me just check your names … we have Hassan, Paul, Sara, Sharon, Louis and Julia. Right? Good, OK, so we'll start by looking at the short assignment I gave you last week. Then we'll spend most of today's session going over this week's lectures. In the last few minutes today I'll give you instructions for the next assignment which is due in next week.

2.9

So, first you need to decide on your focus for the assignment. Then it would be a good idea to divide up the research tasks in your group. Discuss your notes together once you have completed your research. When you've done that, you need to individually write up your reports. Make sure you stay under the 1,500-word limit. Submit the assignments to me by ten o'clock on Tuesday, but before that, one of you should collect all the assignments together, and put them in a folder with your group's name on it. OK … any questions?

UNIT 3

3.1

Part 1

Hello, I'm Dr Andrew Smith, professor of Environmental Studies at Braunton University. Today I'm here to talk about a global event called *Earth Hour* – I'm sure some of you have heard of it, right? Well, the global success of *Earth Hour* shows that ordinary people all over the world really want to stop pollution – by ordinary people, I mean people like you and me. For those of you who don't know, let me tell you a little bit about *Earth Hour* before I explain why I think it is such an important event.

3.2

Part 2

Earth Hour started in Sydney, Australia in 2007. The plan was to use less electricity, to reduce carbon emissions. The idea of *Earth Hour* was simple. Just turn off your lights for an hour. The idea worked. Over 2 million people in Sydney turned off their lights for one whole hour on the evening of March 31st and sat in the dark. It was an incredible sight – dark streets everywhere!

Part 3

And it didn't stop there. In 2008, only one year after it started, 50 million people in 35 countries switched off their lights for an hour. In 2009, hundreds of millions of people switched off in over 4,000 cities. In 2010, there were 126 countries involved, all around the world. Imagine that, all those people switching off their lights and sitting in the dark, talking, laughing … it was wonderful!

Part 4

Why is it growing so fast? Well, because of the media, the papers, television, the internet! Without publicity in the media, people won't join in. Nobody wants to be the only one sitting in the dark! *Earth Hour* had really great publicity. In the world's newspapers and on television there were pictures of famous buildings going dark – I remember seeing Big Ben in London, and the tallest tower in Dubai with its lights off. *Earth Hour* was also on the internet and the radio – everyone was talking about it.

Part 5

But why is it important? It's only one hour a year, after all! Well, it's important because it unites people and makes them think. For that one hour, millions of people are working together to help stop pollution. So this year I will certainly turn off my lights during *Earth Hour*, and my TV, computer, and everything else too. I hope you will too.

Thank you for listening – now, I can see that a lot of you have questions – we have fifteen minutes before …

 3.3

Part 2

Earth Hour started in Sydney, Australia in 2007. The plan was to use less electricity, to reduce carbon emissions. The idea of *Earth Hour* was simple. Just turn off your lights for an hour. The idea worked. Over 2 million people in Sydney turned off their lights for one whole hour on the evening of March 31st and sat in the dark. It was an incredible sight – dark streets everywhere!

Part 3

And it didn't stop there. In 2008, only one year after it started, 50 million people in 35 countries switched off their lights for an hour. In 2009, hundreds of millions of people switched off in over 4,000 cities. In 2010, there were 126 countries involved, all around the world. Imagine that, all those people switching off their lights and sitting in the dark, talking, laughing … it was wonderful!

 3.4

Right, erm, to summarize, *Earth Hour* started in Australia – in Sydney in Australia – in 2006. Lots of people in Sydney turned their lights off for one hour to save electricity. *Earth Hour* has grown very fast and it's now a global event. The first year about two million people turned off their lights – I think that's right – and then every year more and more people joined in … there were over 4,000 cities involved in 2009 … and in 2010 there were 126 countries. Basically, I think *Earth Hour* is a very important event because it shows that ordinary people can make a difference.

3.5

When I was in China last year doing research on the environment, you know one of the most interesting things for me was seeing so many people on bicycles. In China, the bicycle is the main mode of transport for ordinary people. I looked up some numbers, some statistics – did you know there are probably about 800 million bicycles – 800 million – in China! In thousands of towns, hundreds of cities, and in the countryside too, millions of Chinese people travel to work by bike every day. I saw a bike park – like a car park, but for bicycles – with about thirty thousand bikes in it – can you imagine trying to find your bike in that?

3.6

1 There are millions of types of plants and animals on Earth today.
2 There are over 4 million types of insect.
3 The Earth has thousands of types of birds.
4 The Earth has over five thousand types of mammal.

3.7

1 There are about thirteen.
2 It has around sixteen.
3 They have nearly seventy.
4 They have nineteen.
5 There are more than sixty.
6 It has fewer than fifty.
7 It has almost eighteen.
8 There are under fifty.

3.8

Hello everyone. Today's session is the second of our lectures focusing on organizations and the environment. This week we're looking at the World Wide Fund for Nature, the WWF, one of the leading international groups working for the environment. A key area of the WWF's work is in biodiversity. Stop and think for a moment – think of all the different types of plants and animals in the world, the different flowers, trees, animals … this is biodiversity. Biodiversity can be badly affected by humans and the damage we do to the environment.

3.9

The WWF has two main areas of focus. Firstly, the WWF focuses on key places in the world and works towards protecting these. At present, there are 35 of these key places, all very, very important for conserving biodiversity. These places have many forms of life, and also different types of life from anywhere else in the world. A good example of such a place is the Mediterranean region.

The WWF's second focus is on protecting very important plants or animals. These animals or plants could be very important in the environment they live in, for example providing food for other animals. Or these plants and animals could be very important for humans … people like you or me. They could be important perhaps for the business of the local community, or for the health of people in general.

3.10

Let's look in a little more detail now at the Mediterranean region, one of the key areas identified by the WWF for protection. One of the major dangers to the region is tourism. At present, around 220 million people visit the Mediterranean each year. This number, however, is increasing all the time and over the next 20 years, there will be a very big increase, with the number rising to 350 million a year. Many Mediterranean coasts have been very badly damaged already. The coastline of the European Mediterranean is about 46,000km long, and of that 46,000km, more than half now has buildings on. The WWF is working hard to protect the Mediterranean region for the future and at present it has four projects in the region. They are in Croatia, Tunisia, Libya, and Turkey, and they are aimed at protecting the environment and wildlife there. The WWF organization, as you can see, has developed and grown tremendously since 1961, the year the organization started.

3.11

a 34 million people

b 9,000 plants

c 350 projects

d 5 million cars

e 2,725 flowers

f 392 bicycles

g 76 million trees

UNIT 4

 4.1

Well, students, today we have invited two experts to discuss what our homes will be like in the future. To discuss this topic, we have Professor Abdin, originally from Jordan, who teaches architecture at Bell State University, in the United States and Carla Martinez, the well-known Spanish architect who has won many awards for her designs.

 4.2

I = Interviewer   PA = Professor Abdin   C = Carla

I So, Professor Abdin, what do you think houses and apartments will be like in, ooh, let's say the year 2050?

PA This is an interesting question. If you go to Pompeii in Italy you can see what a Roman town looked like 2,000 years ago – surprisingly, you'll find the houses look quite modern. The design of houses hasn't changed much in thousands of years, but in the future, because of new building materials, a growing population, and environmental problems, they are going to be very different.

I OK, so let's start with new building materials. Carla? How will new materials change the way we build houses?

C Yes, I agree with Professor Abdin about the need for buildings to change. I think that houses are going to be easier and cheaper to build because they will use new man-made materials. Since the 1930s, we have seen that man-made materials like plastics, steel, and glass have become more and more popular with architects. Architects in the year 2050 are going to have materials that are easy to use, strong, light, and cheap.

PA I agree.

I Good … now, moving on. The population is growing – what difference will that make to the design of homes? Carla?

C Well, it will make a very big difference. We will need a lot more homes. The United Nations predicts a rise of about 2.5 billion people by the year 2050, so over 9 billion people are going to need homes!

PA That's right. And another point. Those houses are going to have small rooms so that more people can live in each home. A lot of the growing population will be poor, and land to build on is becoming more expensive.

I Right. Now, finally, Professor Abdin, you said that environmental problems will affect the design of buildings.

PA Yes, I think that all buildings will have solar panels to provide electricity … did you know, the Earth gets enough energy from the sun in one hour to produce electricity for the whole world for one year? We must use some of that energy … it would be crazy to waste it!

I Thank you, Professor Abdin and Carla Martinez. Now, for questions …

 4.3

1 The design of houses hasn't changed much in thousands of years, but in the future, because of new building materials, a growing population, and environmental problems, they are going to be very different.

2 I think that houses are going to be easier and cheaper to build because they will use new man-made materials.

3 The United Nations predicts a rise of about 2.5 billion people by the year 2050, so over 9 billion people are going to need homes.

4 Those houses are going to have small rooms so that more people can live in each home.

5 I think that all buildings will have solar panels to provide electricity.

 4.4

1 I love using technology, so I prefer a hi-tech campus.

2 I like a quiet campus, because I don't like too many people around.

3 I like being close to nature, so I like a green campus.

4 I get lost very easily, so I need a small campus.

5 I like busy places with lots to do, so I don't like a quiet campus.

6 I prefer a central campus, because I don't have my own car.

 4.5

1 I love using technology …

2 I like a quiet campus …

3 I like being close to nature …

4 I get lost very easily …

5 I like busy places with lots to do …

6 I prefer a central campus …

 4.6

1 attend a presentation

2 give a summary

3 get information

4 have a break

5 eat in the cafeteria

6 research a topic

7 give an answer

8 ask a question

4.7

Hi everyone. I'm Matthew Evans from the university department of Architecture and Design. I'm here today as part of the series of Career Talks to guide you in choosing your courses for next year. Nice to see so many people here today.

So, why choose architecture? Well, let's start with some facts about studying architecture. The first thing is that we get many different types of people on the architecture course, but every single successful graduate is an imaginative and also a practical person. Secondly, all our students have a love of and a commitment to learning. Another important fact is that studying architecture doesn't have to lead to a career in architecture; it can also lead to careers in many different professional areas. The last fact I'll talk about today is that as an architecture graduate, you can work pretty much anywhere in the world.

4.8

I'm from China. I study at DTU, the Design and Technology University. I'm studying architecture and my courses include Design, Computer Graphics, Physics, Maths and, of course, English

4.9

I loved designing buildings when I was a child so I decided to follow this love and choose architecture as my degree subject. My childhood drawing books were full of pictures of houses. I'm also very interested in the environment and I want to use my architecture studies to design buildings that are environmentally-friendly and green.

I'm doing several courses, including Design, Computer Graphics, Maths and Physics. I have no choice about this. There are some courses which you have to do if you want to be an architect. There is no choice. I chose to do English, because I have to write my assignments and projects in English. Also, our projects have a lot of group work – all in English, of course! Also, when I graduate, the language of the international workplace is English, so that's why I'm studying it!

UNIT 5

5.1

Hello. My name is Gina and I'm the College Counsellor. Today I want to talk to you about becoming good learners, or better learners. Let me explain what I mean by a good learner. Please make notes if you like, and ask questions if you don't understand, OK? To become a good learner, first you need to understand how you learn best – this is called your 'learning style', and that's my topic for today. In this lecture I'm going to focus on three learning styles. OK, the first one we'll look at is called auditory. That's A-U-D-I-T-O-R-Y – auditory. So there's auditory. There's visual, that's V-I-S-U-A-L – visual, and finally, there's tactile, that's T-A-C-T-I-L-E. Has everybody got those names?

Now, let me tell you a little more about each of these learning styles and give you some examples.

5.2

It's clear that we are all different, and we learn differently. Let me tell you about my family. In my family we have three different learning styles. My learning style is auditory. That means I like to learn by listening … for example, if I want to learn how to use a computer, I want someone to explain it to me – I want to hear it!

Then there's my son Eric … he is a visual learner, so he likes to see things to help him learn. For example, if he wants to learn how to use a computer, he likes to read an instruction book. He likes diagrams and illustrations. Then the third type of learner is the tactile learner. This type of learner likes to try things out. My daughter Lily is a tactile learner, so she learns how to use a computer by going' hands on', and sitting at the computer and trying out different things. So, there are three basic types of learners – auditory, visual, and tactile. You are all probably one of these types.

5.3

Now, let's find out which type of learner you are. I'm going to read you 12 statements. You have to listen and then decide if you agree or disagree with each one. If you agree, write A. If you disagree, write D. If you're not sure, write a question mark. OK, so A for Agree, D for Disagree and a question mark for not sure … Does everyone understand? OK. Let's begin.

Remember, A for agree, D for disagree, and a question mark if you are not sure.

Number 1. It is important to study quietly – A, D, or a question mark. It is important to study quietly.

Number 2. You're good at spelling – A, D, or a question mark. You are good at spelling.

Number 3. You dream in colour … you dream in colour.

Number 4. You like to get information from charts … you like to get information from charts.

Number 5. You're good at explaining things … you are good at explaining things.

Number 6. You're good at learning languages … you are good at learning languages.

Number 7. You read slowly … you read slowly.

Number 8. You like to give presentations … you like to give presentations.

Number 9. You take a lot of breaks when you are studying … you take a lot of breaks when you are studying.

Number 10. You like working in a science lab … you like working in a science lab.

Number 11. You're good at sports … you are good at sports.

Number 12. You like making things with your hands … you like making things with your hands.

OK? Now we will find out if you are an auditory, visual, or tactile learner.

5.4

So, now, to find out your score … you get three points for each A answer, 2 points for a question mark, and 1 point for a D answer. You have three totals, one total for questions 1 to 4, one total for questions 5 to 8, and the last total for questions 9 to 12.

5.5

Now, the point of the exercise we've just done is to for you to find out which type of learner you are so you can study in the way that suits your learning style. So let's find out what you are. The first total is for visual learning, the second total is for auditory learning, and so the final total is for tactile learning. Your highest total shows which is your learning style. You may find that you are a mixture of two or more, but usually stronger in one.

5.6

Visual learners need to see things. Good learning activities for them are things like using diagrams, drawing pictures. They should also take lots of notes, and use different colour pens to organize their work.

Auditory learners need to learn by listening, so good learning activities for them are listening to documentaries or other radio programmes. They should try recording lectures and they can also record their own notes after they've made them. Talking in groups is another good way to learn.

Finally, tactile learners need activities with movement, activities which use their hands. They like doing practical classes and going on trips. They should try doing role-plays in class, and also making models.

5.7

1 A Do you know, I really think that a good education is more important than money.
   B Yes, I agree with you. A good education lasts a lifetime, but money only lasts until you spend it!

2 A I know lots of people don't agree, but I think mobile phones should be banned in restaurants.
   B I really don't agree. If you use it quietly, then it's no problem.

3 A Today, we were talking about starting school. In my opinion, children should start school at the age of four. They will have more time to learn to read and write.
   B That's a good point, but I still think it's too young.

5.8

Welcome to today's presentation on learning and intelligence. In this session we're going to explore the theory of multiple intelligences. This is the theory that there are different forms of intelligence, and different people are stronger at different ones. Originally, the theory contained seven different intelligences but now there are eight, which we'll discuss today. However, intelligence number nine has been suggested by Howard Gardner, a Professor at Harvard Graduate School of Education who created this theory.

5.9

So now I'll give you a very short overview of the eight intelligences.

The first intelligence on our list is linguistic intelligence. Linguistic intelligence is the ability to learn languages and to use spoken and written language well. Next we have mathematical intelligence. This means analyzing problems and thinking logically. Mathematical intelligence also means being able to see patterns and to solve problems mathematically.

Number three is bodily-kinesthetic intelligence. This intelligence means being able to use your mind to control and use your body very well, like a footballer who can kick a football very accurately. Spatial intelligence is next. Spatial intelligence is being able to see, use, and make decisions about space and distance, like an architect does. The next intelligence on the list is musical intelligence. If you can recognize, compose, and perform music well, you have strong musical intelligence.

The next two have similar names – we have interpersonal and intrapersonal intelligence. Interpersonal intelligence is having a good understanding of other people and being able to work well in groups, while intrapersonal intelligence is understanding yourself well, knowing what your feelings are and how to control yourself. The final intelligence on our list is naturalist intelligence. This is being good at recognizing and naming things in the environment.

So to recap, the eight intelligences are: linguistic, mathematical, bodily-kinesthetic, spatial, musical, interpersonal, intrapersonal and, finally, naturalist.

UNIT 6

6.1

Bicycle ambulances consist of special two-wheeled trailers and a bicycle. They can transport two passengers, the patient and a family member to look after them, while someone else pedals the bike. It's a very simple idea using very simple technology, but it is really effective and is making a huge difference to many people's lives!

6.2

Well, the bar code is a very simple digital code. It can be read quickly and automatically by a machine – to be precise, a hand-held scanner. The scanner is small and easy to use. Before the bar code, the shop assistant had to ring up every item in a supermarket shopping trolley by hand. It took a long time, and time is money! It also meant that the shop needed many assistants to serve the customers. Both these problems are solved in one quick scan!

R = Richard   AR = Arda   AL = Alison

R Hello, I'm Richard Johns, presenter of the University of Sedworth podcast for Design and Technology students. This week, we set students the challenge of researching and writing a report on a simple piece of technology that has made a positive difference to the world. On today's podcast we have the two winning students. They are here to describe and justify their choice of technology. So, let's turn now to Arda, Arda Soysal, a third year student majoring in Product Design. Hello and welcome to the programme, Arda.

AR Thank you.

R So, Arda, tell us about your choice.

AR Well, I chose a bicycle ambulance. These bicycle ambulances help solve a common but very serious problem in developing countries. How do you get someone to hospital when they are ill or injured? Hospitals are usually quite far from the remote villages where people live, ambulances are expensive, and there are often no good roads for them. So someone had the clever idea of 'bicycle ambulances'. These consist of special two-wheeled trailers and a bicycle. They can transport two passengers, the patient and a family member to look after them, while someone else pedals the bike. It's a very simple idea using very simple technology, but it is really effective and is making a huge difference to many people's lives!

R And how much do they cost?

AR They cost around a hundred dollars each to manufacture. Bicycle ambulances last for years because they are very simple and strong and easy to mend if anything breaks. They are also very reliable.

R So these bicycle ambulances make a big difference. Thanks very much, Arda. Now, let's move on to the second winner, Alison Swift. Alison, can you tell us which technology you have chosen?

AL Well, the technology I chose is very different from Arda's choice. We see it every day, on hundreds, thousands of objects. Of course, I'm talking about the bar code.

R The bar code – an interesting choice, Alison. Can you give our listeners a brief history of this technology?

AL Yes, of course. Well, the bar code is, in fact, quite modern. The first commercial use was in a supermarket in Ohio in 1974 and now it's used by almost every supermarket globally.

R And why did you choose the bar code as the best piece of simple technology?

AL Well, the bar code is a very simple digital code. It can be read quickly and automatically by a machine – to be precise, a hand-held scanner. The scanner is small and easy to use. Before the bar code, the shop assistant had to ring up every item in a supermarket shopping trolley by hand. It took a long time, and time is money! It also meant that the shop needed many assistants to serve the customers. Both these problems are solved in one quick scan!

R So it saves time and money for shops?

AL Yes, and the other big benefit for the shops is that stock control is automatic.

R What about the cost?

AL It's actually very cheap– you can create about twenty bar codes for one US dollar.

R So finally, Alison, can you summarize why the bar code is the best piece of simple technology.

AL Mainly because of its universal impact. We all go shopping, don't we? And as I said earlier, time is money. The bar code saves consumers, shop workers, and businesses time every day. In some shops, it even means customers can scan and check out their own items. It's simple, it's cheap, it's useful – I think it's the best.

OK, thanks Arda and Alison. It's been very interesting to hear about the two different uses of technology and how these help people. But now it's time for you, our listeners, to decide which is better … bar codes or bicycle ambulances. The criteria are: impact on our lives, value for money, and usefulness. So which of the two technologies has had the biggest impact on people's lives? Which is the best value for money? And which is the most useful?

As you can see, there are many internet users in the world now. The first figure shows the number of users in 2009 – approximately 1,800 million worldwide. This number is much bigger than the number of users in 2000 – 360 million. So, according to statistics the number of internet users in the world is growing quickly.

1 We need to find a solution quickly.

2 The main problem we're facing is the number of people.

3 Together we can solve the problem.

4 Solar power could be an effective solution.

5 We must start looking for a solution.

a Today I'm going to talk to you about modern fabrics. In the past, clothes were made from natural fabrics, for example cotton and wool, but now we have the technology to make new fabrics.

b I'm here today to discuss some modern breakthroughs in technology, for example space travel, electric cars, and the internet.

c The topic of my presentation is the use of technology in agriculture, for example, how science helps farmers produce more food, and bigger, healthier animals.

I'm here today to talk about worldwide telephone use, and I would like to start with this slide 'Fixed phone lines in 2010'. This slide shows us the percentage of populations around the world with fixed lines in 2010, that is to say, how many people in different parts of the world were still using telephones in their houses and offices in 2010.

According to statistics, Europe was by far the largest user of landlines in 2010, with 40% of the population having them. The second figure refers to the Americas, a group of developed and less developed countries. The overall figure for the Americas was 28%. This percentage is then cut in half for Asia and the Pacific, which saw only 14% of its population with fixed lines. The Arab countries came next with 9% and finally Africa, with only 1.5 percent of its population having fixed lines in 2010.

6.10

These bicycle ambulances help solve a common but very serious problem in developing countries. How do you get someone to hospital when they are ill or injured? Hospitals are usually quite far from the remote villages where people live, ambulances are expensive, and there are often no good roads for them.

UNIT 7

 7.1

Good morning everyone. My name is Dr Harper, and I'm a lecturer from the Cultural Studies Department. My research area is how culture changes over time, particularly in relation to language. I'm going to talk to you about English as a global language. First of all, I'll talk about the importance of learning English, and after that I'll look at the dangers of having a global language. Next, I'll talk about bilingualism – that is, people who speak two languages – and finally, I'm going to discuss communication issues. There will be time for questions at the end – we'll have about ten minutes, and we're going to have a tutorial together next week to deal with further questions.

7.2

PB = Professor Burchill   DH = Dr Harper   R = Roxanna

PB OK, so is everyone here? Ronesh, Simon, Roxanna? OK, let's get started. As you can see, my colleague Dr Harper, from the Cultural Studies Department, has very kindly agreed to participate in today's tutorial as a follow-up to her lecture last week on Global English. Thank you very much for joining us, Dr Harper.

DH Thank you, Professor Birchill. It's my pleasure to be here. Thanks for inviting me along to answer your questions. Now, let me just do a quick name check. You're Ronesh, you're Simon, and you're … Roxanna?

R That's right.

7.3

1 over 60

2 23

3 over 90

4 as much as 80

5 600

6 half

7 around one and a half billion

8 approximately 75

9 in the thousands

7.4

PB = Professor Burchill   RON = Ronesh   S = Simon
DH = Dr Harper   ROX = Roxanna

PB Right, let's get started. Now, Dr Harper, the students have some questions following your lecture on English as a global language. Ronesh, could you start?

RON Yes, I was interested in English as *the* global language and I wanted to ask you about the use of English as an academic language. How widely is it used?

DH Well, approximately 75% of articles in international journal publications are written in English. And if you focus only on science, well, that percentage rises to over 90. So you can see if you want to do well in the academic context, you need to be able to communicate your ideas in English very well.

PB Simon, do you have a question?

S Yes. Will the globalization of English lead to many other languages dying out?

DH In my opinion, no. I don't think that this will happen. But that doesn't mean that *all* languages will survive forever. Some languages will die out – this is natural. In fact, we think that thousands of languages have died out in the past. Look at Latin, for example – six hundred years ago all educated people in Europe read and understood Latin, but now where is this language? It died out long before English became a global language.

S But I think you said that there are now around one and a half billion speakers of English, native and non-native. This number is large, and it's growing. Does this mean that people will use their mother tongue less and less and, in the end, just use English?

DH No, it means that more people will use two or more languages. Over 60% of the world's population is bilingual. I think this number will continue to grow.

RON I would like to ask you about the benefits of this globalization of English. In your opinion, what are the benefits of so many people now speaking English?

DH Well, it certainly helps communication, and, of course, it saves money.

S Yes … I suppose that when people meet – for business meetings or conferences – they don't have to pay for translators.

DH That's exactly right, Simon. At some meetings of international organizations half of the total budget can be spent on translation. Take the European Union as an example. It has 23 official languages. Most documents are written in English, French, and German. Just think of the cost of that.

ROX Dr Harper, can I ask a question? In the lecture, you said that air transport and modern technology have made a big difference to the rise of global English. Can you explain this point in more detail?

DH Well, because of air transport, many business people from different countries now have meetings face-to-face with other people who don't speak their language. The language they communicate in is English. With regards to modern technology, let's take the internet as our example. The internet means it is possible to 'meet' and communicate with people all over the world at any time. Again, the common language of communication is English. Statistics show that the amount of internet content in English is as much as 80%.

RON I have another question for Dr Harper …

7.5

a Definitely our parents. They are the people we are closest to, so they influence us the most.

b Festivals and holidays don't change. Well, maybe we get new ones, but the old ones always stay the same.

c Parts of our culture will change because of the new culture we are meeting.

d Well, language changes over the years. It has to, because the world is changing.

e It gets stronger. It becomes more important to us because we are far from home.

f I think we learn culture from the media – TV, the internet, and so on.

7.6

Good morning. Thank you for coming. Today we're going to examine the question, 'What is culture?'. Before I start my presentation, I'll give an outline of what I'm going to cover. First, I'm going to define what I mean by culture. Then I'll talk about my culture. Next, I'll discuss other cultures. Finally, I'll talk about common factors between different cultures. At the end, we'll have time for questions.

7.7

1 Some elements of American and European society are the same.

2 The modern world is changing quickly.

3 There are many young people in the Urdu-speaking community in Britain.

7.8

Today's podcast is on the topic of multilingualism. This topic is becoming increasingly important in today's society. So the question we will discuss today is just what does it mean to live in a multilingual world? To discuss this question, with me today are Dr Hamad and Professor Johnson from Stockton University. They study issues faced by multilingual communities and find solutions for particular problems. They recently published a book listing many of their solutions, a book I highly recommend if you want to learn more about multilingualism or you need to study this area for your own research.

7.9

a 15

b three

c over 130 million

d 26

e 24

f around 2,000

7.10

R = Ronesh   DH = Dr Harper

R Yes, OK, but why is English the global language? It's not the most beautiful language and it has difficult spelling …

DH Well, beauty is very subjective and it's true English spelling can be a nightmare, but all languages are different and have their own difficulties – Japanese, spoken by over 130 million people, seems quite easy in some ways. For example, it has only a few vowel sounds, 15 consonant sounds and no articles. Compare this with English, which has many more vowel sounds, 24 consonant sounds, and three articles. However, Japanese has 3 different systems of writing, all of which seem very difficult to an English speaker. At school, Japanese children have to learn around 2,000 kanji symbols for just one of the systems! How many letters are there in the English alphabet? Only 26 … everyone always thinks that their language is the most difficult or best, but in fact children all over the world learn their language in about the same time at the same age and, it would seem, in the same way …

R I see … so really languages are about the same in difficulty …

7.11

Today I'm going to talk about language and culture. Before I start, I'll give an outline of the presentation. First, I'm going to talk about the importance of language. After that, I'll discuss culture. Finally, we'll look at some examples of the connection between language and culture. In next week's tutorial we'll discuss some of the points in more detail.

UNIT 8

8.1

J = Janet   B = Brian

J Good morning listeners, and welcome to 'Top 3'. Today we are very happy to have Brian Davies, professor of City Planning at Newland University, to talk about his top 3 cities. Welcome!

B Thank you, Janet. Well, I found this an extremely difficult task. There are so many remarkable cities in the world. To help myself with this task, I decided to choose three different criteria: I decided to choose one city that is the best for history, or the past. My second city is, I think, the best to show change, so it's best for the present. And my third city is the best for the environment, so it's the best for the future of our planet! So, with these as my criteria, I chose the three cities. So I am going to talk about, first, Rome, which, in my opinion, is the best city for history. Then I'll discuss Dubai, which I think is the best for change, and finally, I'll talk about Copenhagen, which is the best city for the environment.

8.2

J = Janet   B = Brian

B My first city is Rome, capital of Italy, and the best city, in my opinion, for history. Its population is about 2.7 million. It's a very old city, and there are still a lot of old buildings –like the Colosseum, for example, which is almost 2,000 years old. These buildings are important because they show us how people lived then. Nowadays, about 10 million people visit Rome every year, many of them to see the historical sites. Rome is a fascinating city.

My next choice is Dubai in the United Arab Emirates, with a growing population of around 2.2 million. This city is the best to demonstrate change and development. Only about 60 years ago Dubai was just a small trading town. Now, it is a thriving international commercial centre, it has a new transport system – the metro – and many impressive new buildings, for example the Burj Khalifa, which opened in January 2010 and is 828 metres high! Dubai is working hard to develop one of its main resources – its people. Only 40 years ago the adult literacy level in Dubai was lower than 50%. Now it is over 80%, and most of Dubai's university level teaching is in English.My final choice, Copenhagen, capital of Denmark, is a city of about 1.7 million people, and for me it represents the best in terms of environmental responsibility. Statistics show that it's a truly green city. In Copenhagen, most people use public transport or bicycles – 20 % of all journeys are made on bicycles. The city is growing in fame for its green buildings. The 'Green Lighthouse', part of the University of Copenhagen, is carbon neutral – that means it doesn't cause any pollution. The city also provides more than 2,000 bicycles for visitors to use free – there is no charge at all. For the future of our planet, I think all cities need to copy Copenhagen.

So these are my top 3. I believe that from these cities we can learn about our past, our present, and our future. I do hope the listeners get a chance to visit them one day!

J Thank you so much for being on our programme today, Brian, and for sharing some fascinating facts with our listeners.

 8.3

a Rome, the capital of Italy, has a population of almost three million. Brian said that, in his opinion, it's the best city for history. People first lived there thousands of years ago. There are still a lot of old buildings from Roman times like the Colosseum, so we can see how people lived two thousand years ago. These buildings are really important because they show us how people lived in the past.

b He talked about Dubai. It is small, I think he said, and it is sixty years old. There are few roads – he said something about transport. It has a tall tower – I can't remember the name, sorry – it's 800 or 8,000 metres tall I think.

c Brian said that Copenhagen is the capital of Denmark and has 1.7 million people. It's green, clean, and safe, for example, many people use public transport there to go to work instead of using their car. The city also has 2,000 bicycles for visitors to use for free. It's a very clean city. It has environmentally-friendly buildings such as the 'Green Lighthouse'. Brian says all cities should copy Copenhagen.

8.4

A I think we should focus on Istanbul and Berlin for our presentation. I'm interested in the relationships between global cities and I've been researching something called 'town twinning'.

B What's town twinning?

A It's when two towns or cities from different countries form a close relationship and call themselves 'twin towns'. It's a relationship that can last for years or centuries even.

B Oh yes, I think I have heard about that. Is it sometimes called 'sister cities'?

A Yes, that's right. That's the American term for 'twin towns'.

B So Istanbul and Berlin are twin towns.

A That's right.

B OK, so we can use that as the focus for our presentation.

8.5

Both Berlin and Istanbul are important world cities. They have been twin towns since 1989. If we compare their populations, we can see that Istanbul is far bigger than Berlin. It has a population of approximately 13 million, while Berlin has a population of 3.4 million.

Istanbul also has far more visitors each year. Over 20 million visit annually, while Berlin receives around 7.5 million visitors.

A comparison of the number of universities shows that Berlin doesn't have as many as Istanbul, but it has more hospitals. The figures for Berlin are 30 universities and 71 hospitals, compared with Istanbul, which has 44 universities and 49 hospitals. The currency of Berlin is the euro and currently, in 2010, one euro is worth slightly less than two Turkish lira.

8.6

Both Berlin and Istanbul are important world cities. They have been twin towns since 1989. If we compare their populations, we can see that Istanbul is far bigger than Berlin. Istanbul also has far more visitors each year.

A comparison of the number of universities shows that Berlin doesn't have as many as Istanbul, but it has more hospitals. The currency of Germany is the euro and, in 2010, one euro was worth slightly less than two Turkish lira.

8.7

a I've got a research project on cities in Asia. I need to look at cities with a high population and lots of industry.

b I'm giving a presentation on some of the cities in South America next week. I'm going to focus on cities which get a lot of money from tourism.

c The lecturer told us to research the number of people who live in the capitals of the countries in Europe.

8.8

The presentation yesterday was very interesting. The main theme was 'Sport and cities', and the speaker talked about three different cities in relation to sport. First he talked about the annual London marathon. He gave a lot of detail on the organisation of the race. Then he talked about Milan and football. Football is very important for Italians, especially for the people of Milan. Finally, he discussed Beijing and the impact of cycling on the city.

8.9

I am going to compare Moscow and Mexico City. Both Moscow and Mexico City are very interesting cities to visit. Mexico City is in South America, but Moscow is in Europe. Both Mexico City and Moscow are capital cities, but the population of Moscow is not as big as the population of Mexico City. Mexico City is not as cold as Moscow; in fact, the average winter temperature in Mexico is as high as the average summer temperature in Moscow.

UNIT 9

9.1

Good morning, everyone. In today's lecture we're going to explore the brain and memory. I must tell you, I like my lectures to be quite interactive and I expect my audience to answer questions, offer their ideas, and do tasks. So, be prepared! In today's lecture, I will ask some key questions: How are learning and memory connected? What kinds of memory are there? And, finally, how can we improve our memory?

9.2

Before we start, I'd like to review some facts and figures we covered in last week's lecture. Reviewing is one of the key factors for retaining or remembering information. By reviewing these facts and figures now from last week's lecture, you are embedding them more into your memory, and they should stay there for longer. We'll then go on to talk more about the importance of reviewing in helping you to learn.

9.3

Let's look at some brain facts. The human brain is divided into two parts – two hemispheres. These are divided into smaller parts called lobes. Different lobes are responsible for different areas of brain work There are approximately 100 billion nerve cells in our brains. Our brain is a very important organ. It takes up only 2% of our overall body weight, but it uses 20% of our oxygen and blood. The brain is very powerful … and very hungry!

9.4

Now, how are learning and memory connected? People often confuse the two ideas. Learning is the taking in of information. Having memories is expressing this information – by talking or thinking about it, or using it. This diagram represents the relationship between the two concepts, learning and memory. Learning is taking in something new. Memory is remembering past learning or experience.

9.5

Now, there are two main kinds of memory – long-term and short-term. There is also a sensory memory, and some researchers talk about 'working memory'. But today let's focus on short-term memory, then on long-term memory. In the last part of the lecture we will focus on problems with memory and ways to improve memory.

9.6

Short-term memory is the place where we keep information temporarily. Your short-term memory holds information for less than a minute, then it disappears. If we want to keep the information, we need to make an effort to learn it. Short-term memory is very limited in size. It holds only about seven items. In the 1950s, the psychologist George Miller, wrote a very important paper on the subject. He created 'Miller's Law' which argues that seven is the usual number of items a person can remember. Let's look now at long-term memory. This memory is very powerful. It stores information for months, for years even, and it can store large quantities of information. Our long-term memory helps us to remember events – things that happened in the past. It helps us to remember language – how to use and understand words. And it also helps us to remember physical skills – how to swim, and ride a bicycle.

9.7

Now, let's do a little experiment to test Miller's Law – that we can only remember seven items. I'm going to say some numbers. I'm only going to say them once. Listen and, when I tell you, write down the numbers. Ready? The first numbers are … 5 7 3 8. OK, write them down.

Now, for the next numbers … try these … 6 4 9 1 3 2. Write them down. Still OK? Right, a little bit more difficult this time … 5 2 8 4 3 9 6. Write them down. OK …?

Finally …6 3 8 9 1 7 5 6 4. Write them down. Who managed to write all those numbers down? Only a few of you. It was much more difficult, wasn't it? Why? Well, that's Miller's Law in action

9.8

There are problems with both types of memory. With the long-term memory, the brain can change memories over time. Also, some research shows that as we get older our long-term memory gets worse. We don't have these problems with the short-term memory. The problem with the short-term memory is that we need to make an effort to keep the information it can store, or it will be lost forever. To improve our short-term memory, we can actually trick it. If we take our example of numbers – you can remember more digits if you divide the numbers into groups. For example, don't try to remember 3 4 7 3 2 8 6 4 2 1 9 5 – that's 12 digits. Remember it this way, instead: 347 328 642 195.

9.9

So, how can you apply this information about short-term and long-term memory in your studies? First, you have to make the effort to move information from your short-term memory into your long-term memory. Then you have to get information to stay in your long-term memory. The best way to do this is to 'review' it. Research shows that our brain forgets things it thinks are unimportant. By reviewing information, you are telling your brain that this information is important and that you shouldn't forget it. So you should review it later in the day you first studied it. Then again the next day. And then again at the end of the week. This spaced review is very effective for moving information into the long-term memory and keeping it there.

9.10

Another way you can help your long-term memory is by taking good notes. You need good notes to be able to review effectively. Taking notes helps us to remember the information later. When we take notes, we have to think about what we are listening to or reading. We must listen for the key words, and write them down. We have to organize the information in note form. This helps us remember it. Our notes can use visual prompts, for example, coloured pens or highlighters – we remember colours much better than black and white. Good notes don't have to be only words. They can contain diagrams and pictures to help you visualize the information and remember it.

9.11

Today's presentations are all about extraordinary people. There are many people who are good at things, for example, maths or music, but some people are so good that they seem to be almost incredible. I'm going to talk about a famous case of a person with an extraordinary memory. I'm going to talk about 'S'. First, I'll give you the background to his life, then I'll describe his condition and give some examples of the things he could do.

9.12

'S' was a Russian newspaper reporter, living in the first part of the twentieth century. People at work started to notice him because of his memory. For example, when the editor of the newspaper talked to the reporters, 'S' never took notes. He remembered everything. He also invented stories to remember things. He did this by using all five of his senses: sight, hearing, taste, smell, and touch. To give an example, once when he heard a sound, he described it as a brown line on a dark background, with red sides, tasting of soup.

9.13

In this week's lecture I want to talk about another principle, the principle of attention. On your worksheet there are three diagrams – imagine that they show the time of a lecture. Which one do you think shows when we remember things best? Discuss it with your partner. To repeat, which one shows when we remember things best?

9.14

A lot of people think that we start off remembering a lot and then remember less and less until the end. Well, that's not quite true. We do remember a lot at the beginning, and then remember less, but we also remember the end as well as the beginning. We seem to pay more attention, to focus more at the beginning and end of a learning session. This makes some important points: number 1, that we have to be careful to take good notes in the middle of a lecture. The second point is that it means we should work for a short time, then have a break, and then work again. This will help us to remember more …

9.15

1 employer
2 memory
3 learner
4 to present
5 studies
6 research
7 lecture
8 tutor

9.16

For my experiment about learning, I studied two students. In the case of the first student, I found that he can remember faces very well. To give an example, after seeing someone for only a few seconds, he could recognize them easily from a picture. The second student is an example of a person who can't remember faces, but can remember numbers – for instance, he can remember all the telephone numbers of his friends. Another example of his amazing memory is that he can remember fifteen numbers in a row, for instance 328957369238276.

9.17

I will start by asking 'what is the aim of memorization?' Then I will look at three key factors that can help anyone memorize information better. You should take notes on the worksheet, and I will ask you to do some exercises. Please follow my instructions carefully. At the end, you can ask questions and then we will have group discussions.

UNIT 10

10.1

Hello and welcome to Medicine Mode, the University Podcast for medical students. I'm Belinda Little, and joining me today are three experts in the field of gerontology – the study of ageing. First, Dr Carmen Hornsey will give us some facts and figures about health and age. Then Elisabeth Lodge, a research student, will talk about her research into issues involving older people and work. Finally, Professor Clayton Martin will discuss learning and age.

10.2

Hello, and thank you for inviting me onto the programme. I'm Dr Carmen Hornsey, Professor of Gerontology at the Modern Medical University in the UK. In Britain in 1960 there were fewer than 300 people aged 100 or more, but now, in 2011, there are about 6,000, and in 2036 there will probably be 39,000. By 2032, it is predicted that there will be a 61% increase in the number of people over the age of 65 in the UK.

10.3

So, how can we increase our chances of staying healthy into old age? Statistics show that people can lead healthy lives no matter how old they are, if they do four key things – eat well, that means having a healthy balanced diet; do the right kind of exercise for their age, not too much or too little; don't smoke; and have regular medical checkups. Our research conducted in the UK backed up every one of these points.

10.4

Eating well means having a healthy diet, but this means different things for different ages. For example, a teenage boy needs around 2,200 calories a day, while a man needs around 2,550. Older people should have a balanced diet, with at least 5 portions of fresh fruit and vegetables a day and not too much fat, sugar, and salt.

Exercise is the next important factor. Older people should continue to exercise and have a generally active life. You know, in Japan, where on average people live to 81, people in their seventies and eighties still exercise regularly, often walking or cycling every day. Our research showed that in the UK fewer than 20% of people over the age of 65 get the recommended amount of exercise.

Another important factor is, of course, not smoking. Nowadays, everyone knows that smoking is very unhealthy. But, despite this, many people still do it – over 15 billion cigarettes are sold worldwide every day. A person is much more likely to die young if they smoke. Finally, our research highlighted the need for regular medical check-ups to stay healthy. Doctors recommend adults get a full check-up every year. Many medical problems can be stopped if the doctor can treat them early.

10.5

Hello, I'm Elisabeth Lodge. My doctorate is about age and work, so I focused on case studies of older people, some working and some non-working. In Britain, the number of people over the age of 65 will probably rise to above 16 million in the next 25 years. However, at present, the official retirement age is 65, so there are many people over 65 with a lot of time on their hands. Half of my case studies were older people still in employment. The other half had all retired between the ages of 60 and 65. My studies showed that those people who voluntarily stayed in employment were far happier with their lives. In most cases, these people chose to stay in work not for the money, but to stay connected with other people.

One interesting case was a teacher of 68, who retired at 65. After retiring, she reported feeling depressed and lonely. Two years later, she started working part-time in a shop. She reported an immediate and strong improvement in her mental health because of this change in her situation.

10.6

Hello, I'm Professor Clayton Martin, Professor of Gerontology at the University of Wooten. My main research area is the brain and age. What's interesting is that there are many widely held beliefs about the brain and age that just aren't true. For example, it is assumed our memory gets worse as we age. But, in fact, research shows that the brain and the memory can be kept healthy. If we keep our brain active, it can be as good at sixty as it was at twenty. Good activities for the brain are things like reading, learning new skills, and taking up new hobbies.

The essential thing is that we can and should keep on learning new things all our lives. There are many good examples of well-known people who continued working and learning well into old age, people such as the scientist, Einstein, and the painter, Picasso. It is also no longer unusual to hear of a person changing careers later in life, for example becoming a teacher, or starting a business.

10.7

1 So, to sum up, it's time to start taking care of yourself. If you want to stay healthy all your life, start focusing on those things that matter: good food, exercise, medical check-ups – and no smoking! Remember, don't leave it too late. Thanks for listening.

2 So, in conclusion, we can see that it benefits many older people to keep working and contributing to society. And it benefits society too. We must never forget that older people have an important role in our community. Thanks for listening.

3 So my message about learning and age is that it really doesn't matter how old you are – you can continue to grow and develop. There really isn't time to be bored. Life is for learning. Thanks for listening.

10.8

To sum up, this man is one of the most important people in the history of medicine. He lived over a thousand years ago and is often called 'the father of medicine', and I think that this shows he really is the most important. Remember, it all started with him. Thanks for listening. Does anyone have any questions before we finish?

10.9

1 A doctor uses it for listening to the heartbeat of a patient. It's quite small.

2 It's small and it's got numbers on it. You use it to do calculations.

3 It's got headphones. You use it for listening to music.

4 It's quite expensive. You use it to look at very small things.

5 It's electronic. You use it for reading books.

6 Everyone's got one. You use it for talking to people.

10.10

1 Who discovered radium?

2 What did Fleming discover?

3 Who wrote the most important book in traditional Chinese medicine?

4 Who changed the role of nurses?

5 What did Rhazes write?

PHONETIC SYMBOLS

Consonants

1	/p/	as in	**pen** /pen/
2	/b/	as in	**big** /bɪg/
3	/t/	as in	**tea** /tiː/
4	/d/	as in	**do** /duː/
5	/k/	as in	**cat** /kæt/
6	/g/	as in	**go** /gəʊ/
7	/f/	as in	**four** /fɔː/
8	/v/	as in	**very** /'veri/
9	/s/	as in	**son** /sʌn/
10	/z/	as in	**zoo** /zuː/
11	/l/	as in	**live** /lɪv/
12	/m/	as in	**my** /maɪ/
13	/n/	as in	**near** /nɪə/
14	/h/	as in	**happy** /'hæpi/
15	/r/	as in	**red** /red/
16	/j/	as in	**yes** /jes/
17	/w/	as in	**want** /wɒnt/
18	/θ/	as in	**thanks** /θæŋks/
19	/ð/	as in	**the** /ðə/
20	/ʃ/	as in	**she** /ʃiː/
21	/ʒ/	as in	**television** /'telɪvɪʒn/
22	/tʃ/	as in	**child** /tʃaɪld/
23	/dʒ/	as in	**German** /'dʒɜːmən/
24	/ŋ/	as in	**English** /'ɪŋglɪʃ/

Vowels

25	/iː/	as in	**see** /siː/
26	/ɪ/	as in	**his** /hɪz/
27	/i/	as in	**twenty** /'twenti/
28	/e/	as in	**ten** /ten/
29	/æ/	as in	**stamp** /stæmp/
30	/ɑː/	as in	**father** /'fɑːðə/
31	/ɒ/	as in	**hot** /hɒt/
32	/ɔː/	as in	**morning** /'mɔːnɪŋ/
33	/ʊ/	as in	**football** /'fʊtbɔːl/
34	/uː/	as in	**you** /juː/
35	/ʌ/	as in	**sun** /sʌn/
36	/ɜː/	as in	**learn** /lɜːn/
37	/ə/	as in	**letter** /'letə/

Diphthongs (two vowels together)

38	/eɪ/	as in	**name** /neɪm/
39	/əʊ/	as in	**no** /nəʊ/
40	/aɪ/	as in	**my** /maɪ/
41	/aʊ/	as in	**how** /haʊ/
42	/ɔɪ/	as in	**boy** /bɔɪ/
43	/ɪə/	as in	**hear** /hɪə/
44	/eə/	as in	**where** /weə/
45	/ʊə/	as in	**tour** /tʊə/

Great Clarendon Street, Oxford, OX2 6DP, United Kingdom

Oxford University Press is a department of the University of Oxford.
It furthers the University's objective of excellence in research, scholarship,
and education by publishing worldwide. Oxford is a registered trade
mark of Oxford University Press in the UK and in certain other countries

First published in 2011

2015 2014 2013 2012 2011

10 9 8 7 6 5 4 3 2 1

ISBN: 978 0 19 474156 9

Printed in Spain by Orymu, S.A.

This book is printed on paper from certified and well-managed sources

ACKNOWLEDGEMENTS

Illustrations by: Kathy Baxendale pp.14, 25; Melvyn Evans pp.31, 36, 52; Chris
Pavely pp.34, 54; Gavin Reece p.6

*The publisher would like to thank the following for their kind permission to reproduce
photographs and other copyright material:* Alamy pp.4 (students in classroom/
Radius Images); (librarian/Corbis Super RF); 13 (webpage screenshot/Netphotos);
(newspaper/Chris Cooper-Smith); 16 (young businessman/Margaret S); 16 (globe/
beaubelle); 20 (penguins/John moulds); 21 (WWF logo/imagebroker; 22 (Pompeii/
The Art Archive); 37 (mobile phone/Frankie Angel); 37 (MRI Scanner/Caro);
39 (man on phone/Inmagine); (woman on phone/amana images inc.); 40 (two
men/UK Stock Images Ltd); 41 (globe/Petra Roeder); 45 (child doing calligraphy/
Dennis Cox); 48 (Oxford road sign/Geraint Lewis); 51 (marathon/Nathan King);
58 (pilot & student in microlight/Tig Photo); 59 (Pablo Picasso/CuboImages srl);
60 (Mohammad Ibn Zakariya Al-razi/Art Directors & TRIP); 60 (Marie Curie/
Photo Researchers); 62 (e-reader/Kristoffer Tripplaar); Corbis pp.4 (Rutgers
University/Najlah Feanny/Corbis); p.10 (students in Seoul/Kevin R. Morris);
p.11 (portrait of girl/Arabian eye); p.12 (students at lecture/Thomas Imo);
20 (gorillas/Andy Rouse); 20 (air pollution from mill/Mike Grandmaison);
24 (Trinity College/Destinations); 24 (modern University/Dan Forer/Beateworks);
24 (university in Dubai/Georgina Bowater); 29 (boy at laptop/Stephanie Grewel);
34 (early computer/Bettman); 42 (Chinese festival/Christian Kober/JAI/Corbis);
42 (Japanese wedding/Christian Kober/JAI/Corbis); 55 (Tutankhamun coffin/
Robert Harding World Imagery); 60 (Alexander Fleming/Bettman); 62 (microscope/
Duane Osborn/Somos Images); Getty pp.4 (man at lectern/Erik Dreyer);
p.18 (bicycles/Keren Su/China Span); p.19 (polar bears/KEENPRESS); 22 (yellow
building/AFP/Getty Images; 22 (man with books/Nick White); 42 (food/Barbara
Lutterbeck); 42 (The mausoleum of Shah Abdul Latif Bhitta/Iqbal Khatri);
46 (metro train/Bloomberg); 48 (Blue Mosque/David Madison); 48 (Brandenberg
Gate/Andrew Cowlin/Travel Ink); 50 (computer screen/FRANCOIS GUILLOT/
AFP); 58 (men play football/Altrendo images); 60 (Florence Nightingale/Time &
Life Pictures); 60 (statue of Li Shizhen/Keren Su); Oxford University Press
pp.7 (girl in pink/Gareth Boden); 19 (deforestation/Cre8tive Studios); 19 (whale/
Photodisc); 22 (businesswoman/Kevin Peterson); 29 (headphones/Stockbyte);
29 (chemist/Corbis/Digital Stock); 62 (mobile phone/Jason Brindel Commercial);
62 (stethoscope/Photodisc); 62 (calculator/White); 62 (mp3 player/CreativeAct-
Technology Series); Photolibrary Group pp.4 (tutor & student/Alix Minde);
5 (businesswoman studying/Dave & Les Jacobs); 11 (woman/Fotosearch);
19 (traffic in china/TAO images Ltd); 20 (houses on ice cliff/moodboard RF);
25 (architect with model/Paul Hudson); 33 (students in lecture hall/Sabine
Lubenow); 34 (barcode on tin/Diaphor La Phototheque); 35 (barcode scanner/
Corbis); 38 (satellite navigation/Philippe Hays); 46 (Colosseum/Tetra Images);
46 (bikes/SGM); 54 (businessman/Imagesource); 63 (children on grass/John
Lund/Tiffany Schoepp).

*Although every effort has been made to trace and contact copyright holders before
publication, this has not been possible in some cases. We apologise for any apparent
infringement of copyright and, if notified, the publisher will be pleased to rectify any
errors or omissions at the earliest possible opportunity.*